Explore ancient ruins, prist vibrant villag

CORFU

Travel Guide 2025

Kieth T. Ramos

CONTENTS

My Corfu Trip

From the moment I stepped onto Corfu's sun-kissed shores, I was enveloped in a captivating aura of natural beauty and vibrant energy. The island's azure waters, verdant landscapes, and charming architecture painted a picture of idyllic perfection. My journey began with a leisurely exploration of Corfu Town, a historical gem that exuded charm and history at every turn.

Wandering Through Time in Corfu Town

The cobblestone streets of the Old Town, a UNESCO World Heritage site, transported me back in time. The Venetian architecture, with its elegant facades and intricate details, whispered stories of a bygone era. I meandered through quaint squares, each with its own unique character, and admired the historic buildings that lined the narrow alleyways.

The Liston Promenade, a beautiful arcaded walkway, beckoned me with its lively atmosphere. I settled into a cafe, sipping a refreshing drink and watching the world go by. The promenade was a microcosm of Corfu's vibrant spirit, with locals and tourists alike enjoying the sunshine and the lively ambiance.

Exploring Corfu's Historical Landmarks

Eager to delve deeper into Corfu's history, I ventured to the Old Fortress, a massive Venetian structure that stood proudly overlooking the town and the sea. As I wandered through its ancient walls and ramparts, I felt a profound connection to the past, imagining the lives and events that had shaped this historic landmark.

The Esplanade, a vast open space that claims the title of the largest square in Greece, offered a tranquil escape from the bustling streets. I strolled along its pathways, enjoying the fresh air and the vibrant flowerbeds. Nearby, the Saint Michael and

Saint George Palace, a magnificent neoclassical building, housed the Museum of Asian Art, where I immersed myself in the rich cultural heritage of the East.

Basking in the Beauty of Glyfada Beach

A trip to Corfu wouldn't be complete without experiencing its stunning beaches, and Glyfada Beach was a true paradise. The golden sands stretched as far as the eye could see, inviting me to relax and soak up the sun. The crystal-clear turquoise waters were irresistible, and I spent hours swimming, splashing, and enjoying the refreshing embrace of the sea.

I couldn't resist trying my hand at paddleboarding, gliding across the calm waters and enjoying a unique perspective of the coastline. As lunchtime approached, a beachfront taverna beckoned with its enticing aromas of fresh seafood and traditional Greek dishes. I savored a delicious meal, my senses delighted by the flavors and the stunning sea views.

Immersing in Corfu's Cultural Heritage

Corfu's cultural richness is evident in its magnificent palaces and historical estates. The Achilleion Palace, built by Empress Elisabeth of Austria, was a testament to opulence and grandeur. I wandered through its lavish halls, admiring the exquisite furnishings and artwork, and strolled through the manicured gardens, where impressive statues and fountains adorned the landscape.

The Mon Repos Estate, a former royal residence, offered a glimpse into Corfu's aristocratic past. I explored the neoclassical villa, now a museum showcasing the island's archaeological heritage, and wandered through the estate's lush gardens, enjoying the tranquility and natural beauty.

Embracing Adventure and Nature

Corfu's diverse landscapes provide the perfect setting for outdoor adventures, and I embraced the opportunity to explore the island on horseback. In the scenic village of Avlaki, I joined a guided horseback riding tour, traversing through olive groves, forests, and along the coastline. The experience was exhilarating, allowing me to connect with nature and appreciate the island's beauty from a different perspective.

My thirst for adventure led me to Agni Bay, a tranquil haven known for its crystal-clear waters and abundant marine life. I donned my snorkeling gear and plunged into the underwater world, marveling at the colorful fish, sea urchins, and starfish that darted among the rocks and seaweed. The bay was also a playground for water sports enthusiasts, and I enjoyed kayaking and paddleboarding, further immersing myself in the beauty of the Ionian Sea.

Island Hopping and Discovering Hidden Gems

Island hopping is a quintessential Corfu experience, and I embarked on a boat tour to the nearby islands of Paxos and Antipaxos. The journey was a visual feast, with the turquoise waters sparkling under the sun and the coastline revealing hidden coves and secluded beaches.

The Blue Caves of Paxos were a highlight of the tour, their mesmerizing rock formations and vibrant blue waters creating a surreal and unforgettable spectacle. On Antipaxos, I basked in the beauty of Voutoumi Beach and Vrika Beach, their pristine sands and crystal-clear waters inviting me to swim, relax, and soak up the idyllic surroundings.

Exploring Traditional Villages and Savoring Local Flavors

Corfu's traditional villages offer a glimpse into the island's authentic charm and cultural heritage. In Paleokastritsa, I visited the historic Monastery of Paleokastritsa, perched on a hilltop overlooking the bay, and explored its beautiful gardens and chapels. The village's beaches were equally captivating, with their turquoise waters and dramatic cliffs.

A scenic drive to Angelokastro, a Byzantine castle perched on a steep hilltop, rewarded me with breathtaking panoramic views of the island and the sea. I savored lunch at a local taverna in the nearby village of Lakones, enjoying traditional Greek dishes and the warm hospitality of the locals.

In the charming fishing village of Kassiopi, I dined at a waterfront restaurant, enjoying fresh seafood and the picturesque harbor views. The laid-back ambiance and friendly atmosphere of the village made it a perfect place to unwind and soak up the local culture.

Embracing the Nightlife and Saying Farewell

Corfu's nightlife scene is as diverse and vibrant as the island itself. Corfu Town came alive in the evenings, with bars, clubs, and live music venues offering a lively and energetic atmosphere. I enjoyed cocktails and danced the night away, embracing the island's festive spirit.

As my time in Corfu drew to a close, I spent a final day exploring Sidari and the iconic Canal d'Amour, a natural channel carved by the sea through sandstone cliffs. The legend of the channel of love added a touch of romance to my final moments on the island, and the golden sands of Sidari Beach provided a peaceful setting for reflection.

Shopping for souvenirs and local products in Corfu Town was a delightful way to remember my trip. Specialty food stores offered a variety of delicious treats, from kumquat products and olive oil to honey and traditional sweets. I couldn't leave without purchasing some of these culinary treasures to take home and share with loved ones.

My farewell dinner was a celebration of the incredible experiences and memories I had made during my time in Corfu. Savoring gourmet Mediterranean cuisine at a fine dining restaurant, I reflected on the beauty, culture, and adventure that had defined my journey. The enchanting island of Corfu had left an indelible mark on my heart, and I knew that I would carry the memories of this magical trip with me forever.

Discovering Corfu
Historical Highlights

Ancient Echoes and Mythological Origins

Corfu's history stretches back to the mists of time, with archaeological evidence suggesting human presence as early as the Paleolithic era. The island's name, Kerkyra in Greek, is believed to be derived from the nymph Korkyra, a figure in Greek mythology who was said to have been abducted by Poseidon, the mighty god of the sea. This mythological connection hints at the island's enduring relationship with the sea, its strategic location making it a vital maritime hub throughout history.

The ancient Greeks recognized Corfu's strategic importance and established colonies on the island, recognizing its potential as a trading center and naval power. By the 8th century BCE, Corfu had emerged as a significant player in the Greek world, its influence extending across the Ionian Sea and beyond.

The island's naval prowess was demonstrated in 664 BCE when Corfu became the first Greek city-state to challenge the dominance of Corinth in a significant naval engagement. This conflict marked the beginning of Corfu's rise as a maritime power, its skilled sailors and strategic location contributing to its prominence in the ancient world.

Roman and Byzantine Eras

In 229 BCE, Corfu fell under the control of the expanding Roman Empire, becoming an integral part of its vast territories. The Romans recognized the island's strategic value and utilized it as a naval base, strengthening its defenses and infrastructure. During this period, Corfu experienced a period of relative peace and prosperity, with the construction of public buildings, roads, and aqueducts that improved the lives of its inhabitants.

Following the decline of the Roman Empire, Corfu became part of the Byzantine Empire in the 5th century CE. The island's strategic importance continued under Byzantine rule, serving as a crucial outpost for the empire's naval and commercial activities in the eastern Mediterranean. The Byzantines fortified Corfu, constructing impressive walls and fortifications to protect it from invaders. Remnants of Byzantine architecture, including churches and fortifications, can still be seen on the island today, testaments to the empire's enduring legacy.

Venetian Dominance

The fall of Constantinople in 1204 marked a turning point in Corfu's history, as the Byzantine Empire crumbled and new powers emerged in the Mediterranean. In 1386, Corfu came under the control of the Republic of Venice, a maritime power that would profoundly shape the island's destiny for over four centuries.

The Venetians recognized Corfu's strategic importance and invested heavily in its defenses, constructing impressive fortifications to protect it from Ottoman incursions. The island's Old Town, a UNESCO World Heritage Site, is a testament to this Venetian legacy, its architecture reflecting a unique fusion of Greek, Venetian, and other European influences.

Narrow cobblestone streets, lined with elegant mansions and adorned with wrought iron balconies, evoke the grandeur of Venice. Imposing fortresses, strategically positioned to defend the island, stand as silent guardians of its history. The Old Town's harmonious blend of architectural styles, its vibrant atmosphere, and its rich cultural heritage make it a captivating destination for visitors from around the world.

Ottoman Sieges and Corfiot Resilience

Despite the formidable Venetian fortifications, Corfu faced numerous Ottoman sieges throughout its history. The most notable of these occurred in 1537, 1571, and 1716, when the Ottoman Empire sought to expand its influence in the Mediterranean. However, the islanders' resilience, their unwavering determination to defend their homeland, and the strength of the Venetian defenses played a crucial role in repelling these attacks.

The siege of 1716 stands as a testament to Corfu's indomitable spirit. The Ottoman Empire launched a massive invasion force, aiming to capture the island and establish a foothold in the Ionian Sea. However, the island's defenders, led by the Venetian commander Johann Matthias von der Schulenburg, valiantly resisted the onslaught. After a fierce and protracted battle, the Ottomans were defeated, their forces repelled, and Corfu remained under Venetian control. This victory was celebrated across Europe, and Schulenburg's statue still stands proudly in Corfu Town, a symbol of the island's resilience and its triumph over adversity.

British Protectorate

The fall of the Venetian Republic in 1797 brought an end to Venetian rule in Corfu. The island briefly came under French control, followed by a period of Russian and Ottoman rule as part of the Septinsular Republic. In 1815, the Treaty of Paris established the United States of the Ionian Islands, with Corfu as its capital, under British protection.

The British protectorate ushered in an era of significant reforms and modernization for Corfu. The British introduced modern educational institutions, improved road networks, and established the Ionian Academy, the first university in modern Greece. These reforms laid the foundation for Corfu's development as a cultural and intellectual center.

The influence of British rule is still evident in Corfu's architecture, governance, and educational system. The island's elegant buildings, with their neoclassical facades and spacious verandas, reflect the British architectural style. The British also introduced cricket to the island, a sport that remains popular to this day.

Union with Greece

In 1864, the United States of the Ionian Islands was dissolved, and Corfu, along with the other Ionian Islands, was ceded to the Kingdom of Greece. The union with Greece marked a significant turning point in Corfu's history, as the island became an integral part of the modern Greek state.

Throughout the late 19th and early 20th centuries, Corfu continued to thrive as a cultural and intellectual center, its rich heritage and strategic location contributing to its prominence in the Greek world. The island played a significant role in the Greek War of Independence and subsequent efforts to modernize the nation. Corfu's unique blend of cultural influences, its historical significance, and its natural beauty made it a beacon of Greek identity and pride.

World Wars and the Modern Era

The 20th century brought new challenges for Corfu, as the island experienced the impacts of two World Wars. During World War I, Corfu served as a refuge for the Serbian army and government, escaping the onslaught of the Central Powers. The island witnessed significant military and humanitarian activities, as it became a temporary haven for those displaced by the war.

World War II brought further turmoil to Corfu, as the island was occupied by Axis forces. In 1943, the Italian occupation was replaced by German control, leading to significant hardships for the islanders. The Jewish community of Corfu, with a history dating back centuries, faced tragic persecution during this period, a dark chapter in the island's history.

In the post-war era, Corfu emerged as a popular tourist destination, attracting visitors from around the world with its stunning landscapes, pristine beaches, and warm hospitality. The island's economy shifted from agriculture and fishing to tourism, transforming Corfu into a vibrant and cosmopolitan destination.

Preservation of Heritage

Today, Corfu is celebrated not only for its natural beauty but also for its rich historical and cultural heritage. Efforts to preserve the island's architectural treasures, traditions, and customs are ongoing, ensuring that future generations can continue to appreciate Corfu's unique legacy.

The island's museums, historical sites, and cultural festivals offer a glimpse into its storied past, providing visitors with a deeper understanding of Corfu's role in shaping the history of the Mediterranean region. From the ancient ruins and Byzantine churches to the Venetian fortresses and British-era buildings, Corfu stands as a living testament to the diverse civilizations that have left their mark on this enchanting island.

Best Time to Visit

Spring

Spring in Corfu is a time of rebirth and rejuvenation, as the island awakens from its winter slumber and bursts into a symphony of colors and scents. The landscape transforms into a vibrant tapestry of wildflowers, blossoming trees, and lush greenery, creating a picturesque backdrop for exploration and adventure.

The temperatures during spring, ranging from a pleasant 15°C to a comfortable 24°C, provide an ideal climate for outdoor activities and exploration. Hiking trails, such as those in the Corfu Trail network, beckon adventurers to discover the island's hidden gems, offering breathtaking views of the coastline, the rolling hills, and the verdant countryside. Birdwatching enthusiasts will delight in the abundance of avian life, as migratory birds return to the island, their vibrant plumage and melodic songs adding to the symphony of spring.

Springtime in Corfu is also a time of cultural celebration, with Easter festivities that are among the most unique and spectacular in Greece. The island's traditions blend religious devotion with joyous celebrations, creating an atmosphere of spiritual reverence and communal celebration. Processions wind through the streets, carrying icons and religious symbols, while the air fills with the sounds of traditional music and chanting.

One of the most iconic Easter traditions in Corfu is the Pot Throwing custom on Holy Saturday. At noon, locals hurl clay pots from their balconies, creating a cacophony of shattering pottery that symbolizes the earthquake that occurred at the time of Christ's resurrection. This unique tradition, a blend of symbolism and joyous celebration, is a spectacle that captures the spirit of Easter in Corfu.

Spring offers a unique opportunity to experience Corfu's attractions without the crowds that flock to the island during the peak summer months. This is an ideal time to explore historical sites such as the Old Fortress, a Venetian-era citadel that stands guard over Corfu Town; the Achilleion Palace, a majestic 19th-century palace with stunning gardens and panoramic views; and the UNESCO-listed Old Town, with its labyrinthine streets, Venetian architecture, and vibrant atmosphere.

Summer

Summer is the peak tourist season in Corfu, and for good reason. The island basks in glorious sunshine, with long, warm days and temperatures soaring to an average of 25°C to 35°C. This is the perfect time for beach lovers and water sports enthusiasts to embrace the island's coastal charms and enjoy the refreshing waters of the Ionian Sea.

Corfu boasts some of the most beautiful beaches in Greece, each with its own unique character and allure. Glyfada Beach, with its golden sands and crystal-clear waters, is a popular choice for families and sunbathers. Paleokastritsa, with its dramatic cliffs, hidden coves, and turquoise waters, offers a more secluded and adventurous experience. Sidari, with its unique rock formations and shallow waters, is ideal for families with young children.

The summer months are also a time of vibrant festivals and cultural events that showcase Corfu's rich heritage and traditions. The Corfu Beer Festival, held in early June, is a celebration of local brews and Greek cuisine, offering a lively atmosphere and a taste of the island's culinary delights. The island's nightlife also comes alive during the summer, with bars, clubs, and beach parties providing entertainment well into the night.

Summer is an excellent time for exploring the turquoise waters of the Ionian Sea, with boat tours and sailing trips offering a unique perspective on the island's coastline and its surrounding islands. Discover secluded coves, hidden beaches, and picturesque villages, and enjoy swimming, snorkeling, and diving in the crystal-clear waters.

While summer offers the best weather for beach activities and water sports, it's also the busiest time on the island. Popular attractions and beaches can get crowded, and accommodation prices tend to be higher during this peak season. It's advisable to book accommodations and activities well in advance to secure the best options and avoid disappointment.

Autumn

Autumn in Corfu is a season of serene beauty and harvest celebrations, as the summer crowds begin to dissipate and the island settles into a more tranquil rhythm. The temperatures remain mild, ranging from 16°C to 28°C, and the sea retains its warmth, inviting leisurely swims and water activities.

Autumn is the harvest season for grapes and olives in Corfu, and visitors can immerse themselves in the island's agricultural traditions by participating in wine tours and tastings at local vineyards. Some olive groves also offer tours and olive oil tastings, providing a glimpse into the production process and the unique flavors of Corfiot olive oil.

With fewer tourists around, autumn provides a more relaxed atmosphere for exploring Corfu's cultural and historical sites. The Old Town, with its labyrinthine streets, Venetian architecture, and charming shops, is a joy to wander through, discovering hidden courtyards, artisan workshops, and historical landmarks. Museums and galleries, such as the Archaeological Museum of Corfu, offer fascinating insights into the island's rich history and cultural heritage.

The mild autumn weather is also perfect for outdoor pursuits such as hiking, cycling, and horse riding. The Corfu Trail, a long-distance hiking route that traverses the island's diverse landscapes, remains a popular choice for those seeking to experience the island's natural beauty and its hidden gems.

Winter

Winter in Corfu is a time of tranquility and introspection, as the island settles into a quieter pace of life. The temperatures range from a mild 10°C to 16°C, and while it's not the ideal time for swimming and sunbathing, the island offers a different kind of charm during the colder months.

Winter in Corfu is characterized by a peaceful and tranquil atmosphere, making it an ideal destination for travelers seeking a quiet retreat away from the hustle and bustle of everyday life. Many hotels and restaurants in the more touristy areas close for the season, but local tavernas and establishments in Corfu Town remain open, offering a glimpse into the authentic Corfiot lifestyle.

The island's cultural scene continues to thrive in winter, with the Philharmonic Societies of Corfu, known for their exceptional musical performances, often holding concerts and events. Traditional Christmas and New Year celebrations provide a unique opportunity to experience local customs and traditions, immersing yourself in the festive spirit of the season.

Winter is also a good time for birdwatching, as migratory birds visit the island, seeking refuge in its wetlands and lagoons. Lake Korission, a large lagoon on the southern coast of Corfu, becomes a haven for birdlife, attracting a diverse array of species. Winter rains rejuvenate the island's vegetation, creating a lush and verdant landscape that is perfect for nature walks and exploration.

Getting There And Around

Visa Requirement

Corfu, a captivating island paradise in Greece, welcomes visitors from around the globe. To ensure a smooth and hassle-free journey to this enchanting destination, it's essential to understand the visa requirements that apply to your nationality. As Corfu is part of Greece, which is a member of the Schengen Area, the visa regulations are determined by the Schengen Agreement.

Schengen Area

The Schengen Area is a zone comprising 27 European countries that have abolished internal border controls, allowing for free movement of people between member states. This means that a visa issued by one Schengen country is generally valid for travel to all other Schengen countries, including Greece and Corfu.

Visa Requirements

Whether you need a visa to enter Corfu depends on your nationality.

Citizens of Schengen Area Countries

Citizens of Schengen Area countries do not require a visa to enter Greece or Corfu for tourism or business purposes for stays up to 90 days within a 180-day period. They can enter with a valid passport or national identity card.

Citizens of Visa-Exempt Countries

Citizens of many countries outside the Schengen Area are also exempt from visa requirements for short-term stays in Greece and Corfu. These countries include Australia, Canada, the United States, and many others. These individuals can enter with a valid passport that has at least three months of validity remaining beyond their intended stay. However, it's crucial to check the specific requirements for your nationality, as the list of visa-exempt countries can change.

Citizens of Countries Requiring a Visa
Citizens of countries not included in the visa-exempt list must obtain a Schengen visa before traveling to Corfu. This visa allows them to enter Greece and travel within the Schengen Area for a specified period.

Types of Schengen Visas
There are different types of Schengen visas, depending on the purpose and duration of your visit. The most common types include:

Tourist Visa: For individuals traveling to Corfu for tourism purposes, sightseeing, and leisure activities.

Business Visa: For individuals traveling for business-related activities, such as meetings, conferences, or negotiations.

Visiting Family or Friends Visa: For individuals visiting family members or friends residing in Corfu.

Study Visa: For individuals enrolled in educational programs in Corfu.

Schengen Visa Application Process
The application process for a Schengen visa generally involves the following steps:

Determine the appropriate visa type: Identify the specific Schengen visa category that aligns with your purpose of travel.

Gather the required documents: Compile all necessary documents, including a valid passport, completed visa application form, recent photographs, travel itinerary, proof of accommodation, travel insurance, and financial means to support your stay.

Schedule an appointment: Book an appointment at the Greek embassy or consulate in your country of residence.

Attend the visa interview: Attend the scheduled interview, where you may be asked questions about your travel plans and purpose of visit.

Pay the visa fee: Pay the applicable visa fee, which varies depending on your nationality and the type of visa.

Await visa processing: The visa processing time can vary, so it's advisable to apply well in advance of your intended travel dates.

Collect your visa: Once your visa is approved, [1] collect it from the embassy or consulate.

Essential Considerations

Financial Means: You must demonstrate sufficient financial means to cover your travel, accommodation, and living expenses during your stay in Corfu. This can be proven through bank statements, credit card statements, or other financial documents.

Accommodation: You must provide proof of accommodation for your stay in Corfu, such as hotel reservations or a letter of invitation from a host.

Flight Itinerary: You must present a confirmed round-trip flight itinerary, indicating your entry and exit dates from the Schengen Area.

Purpose of Visit: Be prepared to clearly explain the purpose of your visit to Corfu during the visa interview.

Transportation

Getting to Corfu from Europe

By Air

Corfu International Airport Ioannis Kapodistrias (CFU) serves as the primary gateway for travelers arriving from Europe. The airport is well-connected to major European cities, especially during the peak tourist season, offering a convenient and efficient mode of transportation.

Direct Flights: Numerous airlines operate direct flights to Corfu from major European cities, including London, Paris, Rome, Berlin, Amsterdam, and Vienna. Both full-service carriers like British Airways, Air France, and Lufthansa, as well as low-cost airlines such as Ryanair, EasyJet, and Wizz Air, offer these direct connections. Flight times vary depending on the departure city but typically range from 2 to 3 hours, making it a relatively quick journey.

Connecting Flights: For travelers departing from cities without direct flights to Corfu, connecting flights through major European hubs like Athens, Munich, or Zurich provide convenient alternatives. Aegean Airlines, Olympic Air, and other carriers offer frequent flights from these hubs to Corfu. The flight from Athens to Corfu takes approximately one hour, making it a convenient option for travelers from various European destinations.

By Sea

Corfu's strategic location in the Ionian Sea makes it easily accessible by sea from various European ports. The island's main port, located in Corfu Town, serves as a hub for ferries and cruise ships, offering scenic and enjoyable travel experiences.

Ferries: Several ferry companies operate regular services between Corfu and the mainland ports of Igoumenitsa and Patras. The ferry journey from Igoumenitsa to Corfu is relatively short, taking approximately 1 to 1.5 hours. The longer route from Patras to Corfu takes around 7 hours, providing an opportunity to savor the beauty of the Ionian Sea. Additionally, there are ferry connections to other captivating Ionian Islands, such as Paxos, Lefkada, and Kefalonia, allowing for island-hopping adventures.

Cruise Ships: Corfu is a popular port of call for Mediterranean cruise itineraries, attracting visitors from across Europe and beyond. Cruise ships dock at the port of Corfu Town, allowing passengers to disembark and explore the island's treasures on day trips. The port is equipped with modern facilities to accommodate large cruise vessels, ensuring a smooth and comfortable experience for passengers.

By Land and Sea

Combining land and sea transportation is another viable option for reaching Corfu from various European cities. Buses and trains connect major European cities to the mainland ports of Igoumenitsa and Patras, from where travelers can seamlessly connect to a ferry to Corfu.

Buses: KTEL buses operate regular services from Athens, Thessaloniki, and other cities to Igoumenitsa and Patras. The bus journey from Athens to Igoumenitsa takes approximately 6 to 7 hours, while the journey from Thessaloniki to Igoumenitsa takes around 4 to 5 hours. From Igoumenitsa, travelers can easily board a ferry to Corfu, completing their journey to the island.

Trains: The Greek railway network connects Athens and Thessaloniki to the port city of Patras. From Patras, travelers can take a ferry to Corfu, enjoying a scenic journey across the Ionian Sea. The train journey from Athens to Patras takes approximately 3 hours, followed by a 7-hour ferry ride to Corfu.

From North America

By Air

Travelers from North America can reach Corfu by taking connecting flights through major European hubs. While direct flights from North America to Corfu are not available, several airlines offer convenient connections, ensuring a smooth and efficient journey.

Connecting Flights via Europe: Major airlines such as Delta, American Airlines, United Airlines, and Air Canada operate flights from North American cities like New York, Toronto, Chicago, and Los Angeles to European hubs such as London, Paris, Frankfurt, and Rome. From these hubs, travelers can easily connect to Corfu with airlines like Aegean Airlines, Ryanair, EasyJet, and others. The total travel time, including layovers, typically ranges from 10 to 15 hours, depending on the routing and layover duration.

By Sea

While traveling to Corfu entirely by sea from North America is less common, some travelers may choose to include Corfu as a stop on a transatlantic cruise. Several cruise lines offer itineraries that include Mediterranean destinations, including Corfu. Travelers can embark on these cruises from ports in North America, such as New York or Miami, and enjoy a leisurely journey across the Atlantic with stops at various European ports, including the captivating island of Corfu.

From Asia and the Middle East

By Air

Travelers from Asia and the Middle East can reach Corfu by taking connecting flights through major European hubs. Several airlines offer convenient connections to Corfu, ensuring a seamless travel experience.

Connecting Flights via Europe: Major airlines such as Emirates, Qatar Airways, Turkish Airlines, and Etihad Airways operate flights from cities like Dubai, Doha, Istanbul, and Abu Dhabi to European hubs such as Athens, London, Paris, and Frankfurt. From these hubs, travelers can connect to Corfu with airlines like Aegean Airlines, Ryanair, EasyJet, and others. The total travel time, including layovers, typically ranges from 10 to 15 hours, depending on the routing and layover duration.

By Sea

Traveling to Corfu entirely by sea from Asia and the Middle East is uncommon, but some travelers may choose to include Corfu as part of a Mediterranean cruise. Several cruise lines offer itineraries that include Mediterranean destinations, including Corfu. Travelers can embark on these cruises from ports in the Middle East, such as Dubai or Abu Dhabi, and enjoy a leisurely journey with stops at various European ports, including the enchanting island of Corfu.

From Australia and New Zealand

By Air

Travelers from Australia and New Zealand can reach Corfu by taking connecting flights through major European or Middle Eastern hubs. While direct flights from Australia or New Zealand to Corfu are not available, several airlines offer convenient connections, ensuring a smooth journey.

Connecting Flights via Europe or the Middle East: Major airlines such as Qantas, Emirates, Qatar Airways, and Singapore Airlines operate flights from cities like Sydney, Melbourne, Brisbane, and Auckland to European and Middle Eastern hubs such as Dubai, Doha, Singapore, London, and Frankfurt. From these hubs, travelers can connect to Corfu with airlines like Aegean Airlines, Ryanair, EasyJet, and others. The total travel time, including layovers, typically ranges from 20 to 30 hours, depending on the routing and layover duration.

By Sea

Traveling to Corfu entirely by sea from Australia and New Zealand is uncommon, but some travelers may choose to include Corfu as part of a world cruise. Several cruise lines offer itineraries that include Mediterranean destinations, including Corfu. Travelers can embark on these cruises from ports in Australia or New Zealand and enjoy an extended journey with stops at various global ports, including the captivating island of Corfu.

From Africa

By Air

Travelers from Africa can reach Corfu by taking connecting flights through major European or Middle Eastern hubs. Several airlines offer convenient connections to Corfu, ensuring a seamless travel experience.

Connecting Flights via Europe or the Middle East: Major airlines such as Ethiopian Airlines, EgyptAir, South African Airways, and Emirates operate flights from cities like Addis Ababa, Cairo, Johannesburg, and Nairobi to European and Middle Eastern hubs such as Dubai, Doha, Istanbul, London, and Frankfurt. From these hubs, travelers can connect to Corfu with airlines like Aegean Airlines, Ryanair, EasyJet, and others. The total travel time, including layovers, typically ranges from 10 to 20 hours, depending on the routing and layover duration.

By Sea
While traveling to Corfu entirely by sea from Africa is not common, some travelers may choose to include Corfu as part of a Mediterranean cruise. Several cruise lines offer itineraries that include Mediterranean destinations, including Corfu. Travelers can embark on these cruises from ports in North Africa, such as Alexandria or Casablanca, and enjoy a leisurely journey with stops at various European ports, including the enchanting island of Corfu.

Public Transport

Public Buses
The public bus system in Corfu, operated by KTEL Corfu, is a reliable and affordable way to traverse the island. The network comprises two main types of services: blue buses and green buses, each serving distinct areas and routes.

Blue Buses
The blue buses primarily serve Corfu Town and its immediate vicinity, providing frequent connections between the airport, the port, and various neighborhoods within the town. These buses are ideal for travelers seeking quick and convenient transportation within the urban center and its surrounding areas.

Route 15: Airport to Corfu Town (San Rocco Square): This essential route links Corfu International Airport with the central San Rocco Square in Corfu Town, offering a direct connection for arriving passengers. The journey takes approximately 10-15 minutes, and buses run every 30-60 minutes, depending on the time of day.

Route 7: Corfu Town to Dassia: For those seeking the vibrant coastal resort area of Dassia, Route 7 provides a convenient link. The journey takes approximately 20-30 minutes, with buses departing every 30 minutes. Dassia is renowned for its beautiful beach, exciting water sports activities, and lively nightlife.

Route 2a: Corfu Town to Kanoni: This route connects Corfu Town with the scenic area of Kanoni, a haven for those seeking breathtaking views. The journey takes approximately 10-15 minutes, with buses running every 30 minutes. Kanoni offers stunning vistas of Mouse Island (Pontikonisi) and the historic Vlacherna Monastery.

Route 6: Corfu Town to Benitses: Route 6 provides a convenient connection between Corfu Town and the charming coastal village of Benitses. The journey takes approximately 20-30 minutes, with buses departing every 30 minutes. Benitses is known for its picturesque harbor, traditional tavernas, and inviting beaches.

Green Buses

The green buses extend their reach beyond Corfu Town, connecting the capital with other towns, villages, and popular tourist destinations across the island. These buses offer a gateway to explore Corfu's diverse landscapes and experience its rich cultural heritage.

Route A1: Corfu Town to Paleokastritsa: This scenic route links Corfu Town with the picturesque village of Paleokastritsa, renowned for its stunning beaches, crystal-clear waters, and the historic Monastery of Theotokos. The journey takes approximately 45-60 minutes, with buses running several times a day.

Route B2: Corfu Town to Sidari: For those seeking the unique geological formations and romantic allure of the Canal d'Amour, Route B2 provides a direct connection to the lively village of Sidari. The journey takes approximately 1.5 to 2 hours, with buses departing several times a day.

Route C3: Corfu Town to Kavos: Route C3 connects Corfu Town with the bustling resort town of Kavos, a haven for partygoers and those seeking a vibrant nightlife scene. The journey takes approximately 1.5 to 2 hours, with buses running several times a day.

Route D4: Corfu Town to Agios Gordios: This route links Corfu Town with the charming village of Agios Gordios, known for its beautiful beach and dramatic cliffs. The journey takes approximately 45-60 minutes, with buses departing several times a day.

Tickets and Fares

Public bus tickets can be purchased at bus stations, kiosks, or directly from the bus driver, offering convenience and flexibility for travelers. The fares are generally affordable, with prices varying depending on the route and distance traveled.

Single Tickets: Single tickets are valid for one journey on a specific route, providing a cost-effective option for short trips. Prices for single tickets range from €1.10 to €3.30, depending on the distance.

Daily Tickets: For those planning to explore multiple destinations in a single day, daily tickets offer unlimited travel on all blue and green bus routes. The cost of a daily ticket is approximately €5, providing excellent value for money.

Weekly Tickets: Travelers planning an extended stay in Corfu can opt for weekly tickets, which offer unlimited travel on all blue and green bus routes for seven consecutive days. The cost of a weekly ticket is approximately €20, making it an economical choice for frequent bus users.

Taxis

Taxis are readily available throughout Corfu, offering a convenient and comfortable mode of transportation, especially for shorter journeys or when public transport is not a suitable option. Taxi ranks are strategically located at key points, including the airport, the port, and major tourist areas.

Booking a Taxi

Taxi Ranks: Taxis can be found at designated taxi ranks in Corfu Town, the airport, the port, and other busy areas. Simply approach the taxi rank and wait for the next available taxi.

By Phone: Taxis can be booked by phone through various taxi companies operating on the island. It's advisable to save the contact numbers of a few reliable taxi companies for easy access.

Hotel Arrangements: Many hotels and accommodations offer taxi booking services for their guests, providing a hassle-free way to arrange transportation.

Taxi Fares

Taxi fares in Corfu are metered, with rates regulated by the government to ensure fair pricing. The fare is calculated based on the distance traveled and the time of day, with potential surcharges for luggage, airport transfers, and late-night journeys.

Base Fare: The base fare for a taxi ride in Corfu is approximately €3.50.

Per Kilometer Rate: The rate per kilometer is approximately €1.80 during the day and €2.60 during the night (midnight to 5:00 am).

Airport Transfer: The fare for a taxi ride from Corfu International Airport to Corfu Town typically ranges from €15 to €20, depending on traffic conditions and the exact destination.

Ride-Sharing

While ride-sharing services like Uber and Lyft are not widely available in Corfu, some local apps and companies offer similar services. These apps provide a convenient platform to book rides in advance, track your driver's location, and make cashless payments through the app.

Scooter and Bicycle Rentals

For travelers seeking a more adventurous and independent way to explore Corfu, renting a scooter or bicycle is an excellent option. These modes of transportation offer the freedom to navigate the island's scenic roads and discover hidden gems at your own pace.

Scooter Rentals

Several rental agencies in Corfu Town and other tourist areas offer a variety of scooters and motorbikes for rent. Renting a scooter is a popular choice for navigating Corfu's narrow streets and coastal roads, providing a sense of freedom and agility.

Rental Requirements: To rent a scooter, you'll need a valid driver's license (an international driver's license may be required for non-EU visitors) and a credit card for the security deposit. Helmets are mandatory for both the driver and passenger, ensuring safety on the roads.

Rental Rates: Rental rates for scooters vary depending on the type of scooter, engine capacity, and rental duration. Daily rates typically range from €20 to €40, while weekly rates can range from €100 to €200.

Bicycle Rentals

Bicycles can be rented from various shops and rental agencies in Corfu Town and other tourist areas, providing an eco-friendly and healthy way to explore the island. Cycling is a fantastic way to immerse yourself in Corfu's natural beauty, especially along the scenic routes that wind along the coastline and through the picturesque countryside.

Accommodation Guide

Top Hotels and Resorts

Ikos Odisia

Nestled in the picturesque village of Gouvia, Ikos Odisia is a 5-star all-inclusive resort that redefines luxury and relaxation. This haven of tranquility offers spacious and elegantly appointed rooms, each designed with comfort and style in mind. Guests can indulge in a culinary journey at the resort's diverse dining venues, savoring gourmet creations from around the world, from Mediterranean delicacies to international favorites.

The resort's expansive pool area, with its sparkling waters and comfortable loungers, provides a refreshing oasis for relaxation and recreation. The state-of-the-art spa offers a sanctuary for rejuvenation, with a variety of treatments and therapies designed to pamper and revitalize.

For those seeking an active escape, Ikos Odisia offers a range of activities, including water sports, tennis, and fitness classes. Explore the crystal-clear waters of the Ionian Sea with kayaking, paddleboarding, or windsurfing, or perfect your serve on the tennis court. The resort's fitness center provides a well-equipped space for maintaining your wellness routine, with a variety of classes and equipment to suit different preferences.

Atlantica Grand Mediterraneo Resort

Situated in the serene village of Ermones, Atlantica Grand Mediterraneo Resort is a 5-star haven that embodies elegance and tranquility. The resort's beautifully landscaped gardens, with their vibrant flowers and lush greenery, create a peaceful and inviting atmosphere. The stunning pool area, with its sparkling waters and comfortable loungers, provides a refreshing oasis for relaxation and recreation.

Guests can indulge in a culinary journey at the resort's diverse dining venues, savoring a variety of flavors from around the world. The buffet restaurant offers a bountiful selection of international and local cuisine, while the seafood restaurant tantalizes taste buds with fresh catches from the Ionian Sea. The poolside bar provides a casual setting for enjoying refreshing drinks and light snacks.

For those seeking relaxation and rejuvenation, the resort's spa offers a sanctuary of tranquility, with a variety of treatments and therapies designed to pamper and revitalize. The fitness center provides a well-equipped space for maintaining your wellness routine, while outdoor activities such as tennis and mini-golf offer opportunities for recreation and friendly competition.

Domes Miramare, A Luxury Collection Resort
Perched on a hillside overlooking the mesmerizing Ionian Sea, Domes Miramare, A Luxury Collection Resort, is a 5-star haven that embodies elegance and sophistication. The resort's beautifully appointed rooms and suites offer a haven of comfort and style, with private balconies that provide breathtaking views of the coastline and the turquoise waters below.

Guests can indulge in a culinary journey at the resort's diverse dining venues, savoring a range of international and local cuisine prepared with fresh, seasonal ingredients and culinary expertise. The resort's elegant restaurants offer a sophisticated ambiance for enjoying gourmet meals, while the casual poolside bar provides a relaxed setting for light snacks and refreshing drinks.

The resort's expansive pool area, with its sparkling waters and comfortable loungers, is an oasis for relaxation and recreation. The state-of-the-art spa offers a sanctuary for rejuvenation, with a variety of treatments and therapies designed to pamper and revitalize.

For those seeking a holistic wellness experience, the resort offers activities such as yoga and Pilates, allowing guests to connect with their inner selves and enhance their well-being. Guided tours provide opportunities to explore the island's rich history, culture, and natural beauty, enriching your Corfu experience.

Restia Suites

Nestled in the charming village of Acharavi, Restia Suites is a 5-star resort that offers a luxurious and comfortable stay for families and couples seeking a relaxing and enjoyable vacation. The resort's spacious suites provide ample space and modern amenities, ensuring a comfortable and convenient stay.

The resort's expansive pool area, with its separate pools for adults and children, provides a refreshing oasis for relaxation and recreation. The state-of-the-art spa offers a sanctuary for rejuvenation, with a variety of treatments and therapies designed to pamper and revitalize.

Guests can indulge in a culinary journey at the resort's diverse dining venues, savoring a variety of Mediterranean and international dishes prepared with fresh, local ingredients and culinary expertise. The resort also offers a range of activities, including tennis, mini-golf, and water sports, providing opportunities for fun and recreation for all ages.

Akrotiri Beach Resort Hotel

Located in the picturesque village of Paleokastritsa, Akrotiri Beach Resort Hotel is a 4-star haven that offers a tranquil and relaxing escape. The resort's beautiful beachfront location provides direct access to the crystal-clear waters of the Ionian Sea, perfect for swimming, sunbathing, and water sports.

The resort's comfortable rooms offer a cozy and inviting retreat, while the expansive pool area provides a refreshing oasis for relaxation and recreation. The spa offers a sanctuary for rejuvenation, with a variety of treatments and therapies designed to pamper and revitalize.

Guests can savor a variety of local and international cuisine at the resort's restaurants, enjoying delicious meals with stunning views of the coastline. The resort also offers activities such as snorkeling, diving, and boat trips, allowing guests to explore the underwater world and discover the hidden gems of the Ionian Sea.

Kerkyra Blue Hotel N' Spa

Located in the heart of Corfu Town, Kerkyra Blue Hotel N' Spa is a 5-star urban retreat that offers a luxurious and relaxing experience. The resort's elegant rooms and suites provide a haven of comfort and style, with modern amenities and sophisticated décor.

The resort's expansive pool area, with its sparkling waters and comfortable loungers, provides a refreshing oasis for relaxation and recreation. The state-of-the-art spa offers a sanctuary for rejuvenation, with a variety of treatments and therapies designed to pamper and revitalize.

Guests can indulge in a culinary journey at the resort's diverse dining venues, savoring a variety of Mediterranean and international dishes prepared with fresh, local ingredients and culinary expertise. The resort also offers activities such as yoga and Pilates, allowing guests to connect with their inner selves and enhance their well-being. Guided tours provide opportunities to explore the island's rich history, culture, and natural beauty, enriching your Corfu experience.

Kontokali Bay Resort & Spa

Nestled in the serene bay of Kontokali, Kontokali Bay Resort & Spa is a 5-star haven that embodies elegance and tranquility. The resort's beautifully landscaped gardens, with their vibrant flowers and lush greenery, create a peaceful and inviting atmosphere. The stunning pool area, with its sparkling waters and comfortable loungers, provides a refreshing oasis for relaxation and recreation.

Guests can indulge in a culinary journey at the resort's diverse dining venues, savoring a variety of flavors from around the world. The buffet restaurant offers a bountiful selection of international and local cuisine, while the seafood restaurant tantalizes taste buds with fresh catches from the Ionian Sea. The poolside bar provides a casual setting for enjoying refreshing drinks and light snacks.

For those seeking relaxation and rejuvenation, the resort's spa offers a sanctuary of tranquility, with a variety of treatments and therapies designed to pamper and revitalize. The fitness center provides a well-equipped space for maintaining your wellness routine, while outdoor activities such as tennis and mini-golf offer opportunities for recreation and friendly competition.

Corfu Imperial, Grecotel Exclusive Resort
Situated in the picturesque coastal town of Dassia, Corfu Imperial, Grecotel Exclusive Resort, is a 5-star haven that embodies luxury and relaxation. The resort's spacious and elegantly appointed rooms offer a haven of comfort and style, with private balconies that provide breathtaking views of the Ionian Sea.

Guests can indulge in a culinary journey at the resort's diverse dining venues, savoring gourmet creations from around the world, from Mediterranean delicacies to international favorites. The resort's elegant restaurants offer a sophisticated ambiance for enjoying gourmet meals, while the casual poolside bar provides a relaxed setting for light snacks and refreshing drinks.

The resort's expansive pool area, with its sparkling waters and comfortable loungers, is an oasis for relaxation and recreation. The state-of-the-art spa offers a sanctuary for rejuvenation, with a variety of treatments and therapies designed to pamper and revitalize.

For those seeking an active escape, Corfu Imperial offers a range of activities, including water sports, tennis, and fitness classes. Explore the crystal-clear waters of the Ionian Sea with kayaking, paddleboarding, or windsurfing, or perfect your serve on the tennis court. The resort's fitness center provides a well-equipped space for maintaining your wellness routine, with a variety of classes and equipment to suit different preferences.

Kairaba Sandy Villas

Nestled amidst the serene landscapes of Agios Georgios, Kairaba Sandy Villas is a 5-star resort that offers a luxurious and comfortable stay for those seeking privacy and tranquility. The resort's spacious villas provide a haven of comfort and style, with private pools, fully equipped kitchens, and ample space for relaxation and entertainment.

The resort's expansive pool area, with its sparkling waters and comfortable loungers, provides a refreshing oasis for relaxation and recreation. The state-of-the-art spa offers a sanctuary for rejuvenation, with a variety of treatments and therapies designed to pamper and revitalize.

Guests can indulge in a culinary journey at the resort's diverse dining venues, savoring a variety of Mediterranean and international dishes prepared with fresh, local ingredients and culinary expertise. The resort also offers a range of activities, including tennis, mini-golf, and water sports, providing opportunities for fun and recreation for all ages.

Dreams Corfu Resort & Spa

Located in the picturesque village of Gouvia, Dreams Corfu Resort & Spa is a 5-star resort that offers a luxurious and relaxing experience with a focus on holistic wellness. The resort's elegant rooms and suites provide a haven of comfort and style, with modern amenities and sophisticated décor.

The resort's expansive pool area, with its sparkling waters and comfortable loungers, provides a refreshing oasis for relaxation and recreation. The state-of-the-art spa offers a sanctuary for rejuvenation, with a variety of treatments and therapies designed to pamper and revitalize.

Guests can indulge in a culinary journey at the resort's diverse dining venues, savoring a variety of Mediterranean and international dishes prepared with fresh, local ingredients and culinary expertise. The resort also offers activities such as yoga and Pilates, allowing guests to connect with their inner selves and enhance their well-being. Guided tours provide opportunities to explore the island's rich history, culture, and natural beauty, enriching your Corfu experience.

Budget Friendly Accommodation

Locandiera Hotel

Located in the heart of Corfu Old Town, Locandiera Hotel is a charming and affordable option for travelers seeking a taste of the city's rich history and vibrant atmosphere. Housed in a beautifully restored historical building, the hotel seamlessly blends traditional architecture with modern comforts. Guests can enjoy well-appointed rooms with contemporary amenities, ensuring a relaxing and enjoyable stay. The hotel's central location places you steps away from the Old Town's labyrinthine streets, where you can wander amidst charming cafes, admire the beautiful architecture, and soak in the vibrant atmosphere of this UNESCO World Heritage Site.

Casa Verde

Casa Verde, a budget-friendly apartment situated in the heart of Corfu Old Town, offers a comfortable and convenient stay for travelers seeking a home-like atmosphere. This well-appointed apartment features modern amenities, including free Wi-Fi, ensuring that you can stay connected and entertained throughout your stay. The apartment also provides luggage storage, allowing you to explore the city unburdened before your departure. Casa Verde's central location offers easy access to local attractions, including the Byzantine Museum, with its impressive collection of religious icons and artifacts, and the New Fortress, a Venetian-era citadel with stunning views of the city and the sea.

Roof Garden House

Roof Garden House, located in the heart of Corfu Old Town, offers a unique and affordable stay with breathtaking coastal views. This charming property features a terrace where guests can relax and enjoy the fresh air and sunshine, while free Wi-Fi ensures that you can stay connected throughout your stay. The beachfront location provides easy access to the sandy shores and the crystal-clear waters of the Ionian Sea, making it an ideal choice for those seeking a relaxing beach vacation. The Roof Garden House is also conveniently located near the Ionio University, a historic institution with beautiful architecture, and the Serbian Museum, which houses a collection of artifacts and documents related to the Serbian soldiers who found refuge in Corfu during World War I.

Acanthus Blue Hotel

Acanthus Blue Hotel, situated in the heart of Corfu Old Town, offers a budget-friendly option for travelers seeking a comfortable and convenient stay. The hotel features a garden and terrace where guests can relax and enjoy the fresh air, as well as an on-site restaurant and bar where they can savor delicious meals and refreshing drinks. The hotel's modern amenities and comfortable rooms ensure a pleasant stay, while its location in the vibrant Old Town provides easy access to the city's historical and cultural attractions.

Bonagrazia

Bonagrazia, a charming and affordable hotel in Corfu Old Town, offers a welcoming atmosphere and a convenient location for exploring the city's treasures. The hotel is situated near the Asian Art Museum, which houses an impressive collection of Asian art and artifacts, and the Public Garden, a tranquil oasis in the heart of the city. Guests can enjoy comfortable rooms and a friendly atmosphere, making Bonagrazia a welcoming and affordable choice for budget-conscious travelers.

Old Town Luxury Suites 'Princess'

Old Town Luxury Suites 'Princess' offers a touch of affordable luxury in the heart of Corfu Old Town. The hotel's comfortable suites feature modern amenities and elegant décor, providing a luxurious and relaxing retreat. The hotel's central location offers easy access to local attractions, including the iconic Saint Spyridon Church, with its impressive bell tower and ornate interior, and the Byzantine Museum, which houses a collection of religious icons and artifacts.

Lear Liston Suite

Lear Liston Suite provides a budget-friendly option for travelers seeking a comfortable and convenient base for exploring Corfu Town. The suite's location in the heart of the Old Town offers easy access to the city's historical and cultural attractions, including the Byzantine Museum and the New Fortress. The suite's comfortable accommodations and modern amenities ensure a pleasant and relaxing stay, while its affordable price makes it an ideal choice for budget-conscious travelers.

Suite 16

Suite 16, a recently renovated apartment in the center of Corfu Town, offers affordable accommodation with modern amenities and a convenient location. The apartment's stylish décor and comfortable furnishings create a welcoming and relaxing atmosphere. Its central location provides easy access to local attractions, including the Royal Baths Mon Repos, a former royal estate with beautiful gardens and ancient ruins, and the New Fortress, a Venetian-era citadel with stunning views of the city and the sea.

Muses Luxury Suites

Muses Luxury Suites offers a budget-friendly option for travelers seeking comfortable accommodations and a convenient location in Corfu Old Town. The suites are situated near the Byzantine Museum, the Public Garden, and Saint Spyridon Church, providing easy access to the city's historical and cultural landmarks. The suites' comfortable furnishings and modern amenities ensure a pleasant and relaxing stay, while their affordable price makes them an ideal choice for budget-conscious travelers.

New York Luxury Suites

New York Luxury Suites provides a budget-friendly option for travelers seeking modern amenities and a vibrant atmosphere in Corfu Old Town. The hotel's comfortable rooms and contemporary décor create a welcoming and stylish retreat. The hotel's location near the New Fortress offers easy access to local attractions, while its proximity to the city's vibrant nightlife and dining scene ensures that guests can fully immerse themselves in the city's energy.

Unique Stays

The Merchant's House

Nestled in the heart of Corfu Town, The Merchant's House is a beautifully restored 19th-century mansion that seamlessly blends historical charm with modern luxury. This elegant residence, once home to a prominent merchant family, offers a glimpse into Corfu's rich past while providing all the comforts of a contemporary boutique hotel.

The mansion's elegantly decorated rooms feature antique furnishings, high ceilings, and large windows that flood the space with natural light and offer stunning views of the town's charming streets and historic landmarks. Guests can relax in the tranquil garden, a hidden oasis amidst the bustling city, or enjoy a delightful breakfast in the courtyard, savoring local delicacies and freshly brewed coffee. The personalized service and attention to detail at The Merchant's House create an atmosphere of refined elegance and ensure a truly special stay.

Rou Estate

Situated amidst the rolling hills of northeastern Corfu, Rou Estate is a unique collection of restored stone houses that offer an authentic and luxurious retreat. This idyllic estate, with its beautifully landscaped gardens, panoramic views of the Ionian Sea, and tranquil atmosphere, provides a haven for those seeking a peaceful escape and a connection to nature.

Each house on the estate has been individually designed, preserving its original character and charm while incorporating modern comforts and amenities. Guests can relax by the infinity pool, its turquoise waters blending seamlessly with the horizon, or unwind in the beautifully landscaped gardens, surrounded by fragrant flowers and olive groves.

Rou Estate also offers a range of activities and experiences that cater to those seeking a holistic and enriching stay. Yoga classes, held in the tranquil gardens, provide an opportunity to connect with your inner self and enhance your well-being. Cooking workshops, led by local chefs, introduce you to the flavors and techniques of Corfiot cuisine, allowing you to create delicious dishes using fresh, local ingredients. Guided walks through the surrounding countryside reveal the island's hidden gems, from ancient ruins to picturesque villages.

Mayor La Grotta Verde Grand Resort
Perched on a cliffside in Agios Gordios, Mayor La Grotta Verde Grand Resort offers a unique and luxurious stay with spectacular views of the Ionian Sea. This idyllic resort, with its elegant architecture and breathtaking setting, provides a haven for those seeking a romantic escape or a relaxing retreat.

The resort's spacious and elegantly decorated rooms and suites offer a haven of comfort and style, each with a private balcony or terrace that provides stunning panoramic views of the coastline and the turquoise waters below. Guests can indulge in the resort's spa, where a variety of treatments and therapies are designed to pamper and revitalize. The resort's gourmet restaurants offer a culinary journey, with menus featuring fresh, local ingredients and international flavors.

For those seeking relaxation and recreation, the resort offers a private beach, where guests can soak up the sun, swim in the crystal-clear waters, or enjoy a variety of water sports. The resort's infinity pool, with its breathtaking views of the sea, provides another oasis for relaxation and rejuvenation.

Casa Lucia
Located in the picturesque village of Sgombou, Casa Lucia is a charming and eco-friendly retreat that offers a unique and tranquil

stay. This idyllic property, set amidst lush gardens and olive groves, features a collection of traditional stone cottages that have been lovingly restored and decorated with rustic charm.

Guests can enjoy the serene atmosphere, relax by the pool, and participate in yoga and meditation classes, fostering a sense of inner peace and connection to nature. Casa Lucia also hosts cultural events, workshops, and festivals, providing a rich and immersive experience for its guests. These events, often featuring local musicians, artists, and artisans, offer a glimpse into Corfu's vibrant cultural heritage and its traditions.

Bella Venezia Hotel
Situated in a neoclassical mansion in the heart of Corfu Town, Bella Venezia Hotel offers a unique and elegant stay with a touch of history. This charming hotel, with its beautifully appointed rooms and period furnishings, evokes the grandeur and sophistication of a bygone era.

Guests can relax in the hotel's tranquil garden, a hidden oasis amidst the bustling city, or enjoy a delicious breakfast in the elegant dining room, savoring local delicacies and freshly brewed coffee. The hotel's central location provides easy access to the many attractions of Corfu Town, from the historic Old Fortress and the vibrant Liston Promenade to the charming shops and cafes of the Old Town.

Villas at Bioporos
Located in the serene area of Agios Matheos, Bioporos Organic Farm offers a unique and eco-friendly stay in traditional stone villas. This idyllic farm, set amidst olive groves and vineyards, provides a glimpse into the authentic Corfiot lifestyle, where nature and tradition intertwine.

The villas, beautifully decorated with rustic furnishings and modern amenities, offer stunning views of the surrounding countryside, creating a peaceful and relaxing atmosphere. Guests can participate in farm activities, learning about organic farming practices and experiencing the daily rhythms of rural life. The farm-to-table cuisine, prepared with fresh, organic ingredients grown on the property, offers a taste of authentic Corfiot flavors. Guests can also explore the nearby beaches and nature trails, discovering the island's natural beauty and enjoying outdoor activities such as hiking, swimming, and cycling.

The Venetian Well Hotel

Nestled in a historic building in the heart of Corfu Town, The Venetian Well Hotel offers a unique and luxurious stay with a touch of Venetian elegance. This charming hotel, with its exquisitely decorated rooms and antique furnishings, evokes the grandeur and sophistication of Corfu's Venetian past.

Guests can relax in the hotel's tranquil courtyard, a hidden oasis amidst the bustling city, or savor gourmet meals at the on-site restaurant, enjoying a culinary journey through Corfiot and Mediterranean flavors. The hotel's proximity to the charming streets of the Old Town invites exploration and discovery, with its historic landmarks, artisan shops, and vibrant cafes.

San Antonio Corfu Resort

Located in the picturesque village of Kalami, San Antonio Corfu Resort offers a unique and romantic stay with breathtaking views of the bay. This idyllic resort, with its stylish and contemporary design, provides a tranquil escape for couples seeking a secluded and luxurious getaway.

The resort's rooms and suites, each with a private balcony or terrace, offer stunning views of the turquoise waters and the lush greenery that surrounds the bay. Guests can relax by the infinity pool, its crystal-clear waters seemingly merging with the horizon, or savor delicious meals at the resort's beachfront restaurant, enjoying the fresh flavors of Mediterranean cuisine while soaking in the breathtaking scenery.

Akrotiri Beach Hotel

Perched on a cliffside in Paleokastritsa, Akrotiri Beach Hotel offers a unique and breathtaking stay with panoramic views of the Ionian Sea. This idyllic hotel, with its comfortable and modern rooms, provides a tranquil escape for those seeking a coastal retreat with stunning scenery and a relaxed atmosphere.

Each room features a private balcony that overlooks the mesmerizing turquoise waters of the Ionian Sea, offering breathtaking views that change with the light and the tides. Guests can relax by the infinity pool, its edge seemingly disappearing into the horizon, or enjoy water sports at the nearby beach, exploring the underwater world and embracing the island's coastal beauty.

The hotel's restaurant, with its panoramic views, offers a culinary journey through Corfiot and Mediterranean flavors, with fresh, locally sourced ingredients and culinary expertise.

Major Landmarks

Old Fortress and New Fortress

Standing proudly on a rocky peninsula that juts out into the shimmering Ionian Sea, the Old Fortress of Corfu, also known as Palaio Frourio, is an iconic landmark that embodies the island's rich history and resilience. Its imposing silhouette, with its towering walls and formidable bastions, has witnessed centuries of conflict, cultural exchange, and architectural evolution.

Byzantine Beginnings

The origins of the Old Fortress can be traced back to the Byzantine period, around the 6th century AD, when the initial fortifications were erected to protect the island from invaders. The Byzantines, recognizing the strategic importance of Corfu's location at the crossroads of maritime trade routes, constructed defensive walls and structures to safeguard the town and its inhabitants. These early fortifications, though modest in comparison to later additions, laid the foundation for the fortress that would become a symbol of Corfu's strength and endurance.

Venetian Masterpiece

When the Venetians took control of Corfu in 1386, they embarked on an ambitious project to strengthen the island's defenses, recognizing the growing threat of Ottoman expansion in the Mediterranean. The Old Fortress became a focal point of their efforts, undergoing a dramatic transformation that would shape its identity for centuries to come.

The Venetians, renowned for their mastery of military engineering, constructed massive walls, imposing bastions, and intricate defensive structures, transforming the fortress into an impregnable stronghold. The fortress was designed to withstand long sieges and relentless attacks, its strategic location and formidable defenses making it a crucial bulwark against Ottoman ambitions.

To further enhance the fortress's defenses, the Venetians created a moat, known as the Contrafossa, which separated the fortress from the rest of the town. This moat, filled with seawater, served as an additional barrier against invaders, making the fortress even more formidable. Access to the fortress was controlled by a drawbridge, and its entrance was guarded by imposing gates and towers, ensuring that only authorized personnel could enter.

Architectural Marvel

The Old Fortress stands as a testament to Venetian architectural prowess, its massive stone walls and bastions reflecting the ingenuity and engineering skills of the era. The fortress is divided into two main sections: the outer and inner citadels. The outer citadel, with its network of bastions, walls, and ramparts, formed the main line of defense, designed to withstand artillery bombardment and repel invaders. The inner citadel, more sheltered and secure, housed refined buildings, including churches, administrative offices, and living quarters for the garrison.

One of the most notable features of the Old Fortress is the Church of St. George, a beautiful structure that stands in stark contrast to the fortress's military architecture. Built by the British in 1840, during their protectorate of the Ionian Islands, the church resembles an ancient Doric temple, with its impressive colonnade and classical design. It serves as a reminder of the British influence on Corfu and adds a touch of elegance to the fortress's imposing silhouette.

Historical Significance

The Old Fortress has borne witness to numerous historical events and battles throughout its existence. It played a crucial role during the Ottoman sieges of Corfu, particularly in 1537, 1571, and 1716, when the Ottoman Empire sought to conquer the island. The fortress's formidable defenses and the bravery of its defenders ensured that Corfu remained unconquered, its walls standing strong against the relentless attacks.

During World War II, the Old Fortress served as a shelter for the local population during air raids, providing a refuge from the devastation of war. It was also used by various military forces over the years, including the British, who maintained a presence on the island until 1864.

Today, the Old Fortress stands as a symbol of Corfu's rich history and heritage, a testament to the island's resilience and its ability to withstand the challenges of time. Visitors can explore its labyrinthine passageways, climb its ramparts for breathtaking views of the island and the sea, and delve into the island's past through exhibits and displays that bring its history to life.

The New Fortress

The New Fortress, or Neo Frourio, is another significant fortification in Corfu, situated on the hill of St. Mark, overlooking the city and the harbor. Built by the Venetians in the 16th century, the New Fortress was designed to complement the defenses of the Old Fortress, providing additional protection to the island and strengthening its strategic position in the Ionian Sea.

Venetian Construction

The construction of the New Fortress began in 1576 under the supervision of Michele Sanmicheli, a renowned Venetian military engineer. The fortress was completed in 1645, its design reflecting the advancements in military architecture and fortification techniques of the time. The Venetians, ever vigilant against the threat of Ottoman expansion, sought to create a fortress that could withstand the latest artillery and siege tactics.

Architectural Features

The New Fortress is a sprawling complex of walls, bastions, and underground tunnels, its design incorporating the latest innovations in military engineering to create a formidable stronghold. The fortress is built on two levels, with the lower level housing the main defensive structures, including massive stone walls, reinforced with earthworks and bastions, designed to absorb and deflect artillery fire. The upper level served as a command center and barracks, providing a strategic vantage point for observing the surrounding area and coordinating defenses.

One of the key features of the New Fortress is its network of underground tunnels and chambers, which served a variety of purposes. These tunnels were used for storage, communication, and troop movements, allowing the defenders to move quickly and efficiently within the fortress and maintain their defenses even under siege.

The entrance to the New Fortress is marked by a grand gateway adorned with the emblem of the Venetian Republic, the Lion of St. Mark. This symbol of Venetian power and authority serves as a reminder of the fortress's historical significance and its role in protecting Corfu from invaders.

Historical Significance

The New Fortress played a vital role in the defense of Corfu during the numerous Ottoman sieges, its strategic location on the hill of St. Mark providing a commanding view of the surrounding area and allowing the defenders to spot approaching enemy forces from a distance. The fortress's formidable defenses and its strategic position made it a crucial component of Corfu's defensive network.

The fortress also served as a military barracks, arsenal, and administrative center during the 18th and 19th centuries, contributing to the island's security and governance. During the British protectorate of Corfu, the New Fortress was used by British troops, and various modifications were made to the structure to accommodate their needs.

In more recent history, the New Fortress played a role during World War II, serving as a defensive position and shelter for the local population during air raids. The fortress suffered some damage during the war, but it was subsequently restored and preserved as a historical monument, a testament to its enduring significance.

Liston Promenade

Historical Background

The Liston Promenade's story begins in the early 19th century during the French occupation of Corfu. Between 1807 and 1814, under the administration of General Mathieu de Lesseps, a French officer with a vision for urban renewal, the promenade took shape. Inspired by the Rue de Rivoli in Paris, a grand boulevard lined with arcaded buildings, the Liston was designed to embody the neoclassical architectural style that was sweeping across Europe at the time.

The name Liston is believed to be derived from the Italian word lista, which referred to a long, narrow strip of land. This aptly describes the promenade's elongated form, stretching along the edge of the Spianada, Corfu Town's expansive central square. The Liston was envisioned as a grand and elegant walkway, a place where the island's elite and aristocracy could gather, stroll, and engage in social discourse. Its design was intended to enhance the urban landscape of Corfu Town, providing a picturesque and sophisticated setting for public life.

Architectural Features

The Liston Promenade is characterized by its distinctive arcades, a series of elegant arches and columns that support the buildings lining the walkway. These arcaded structures, with their classical architectural elements, create a sense of timeless beauty and grandeur. Pilasters, cornices, and balustrades adorn the facades, adding to the promenade's refined aesthetic.

The buildings themselves are adorned with large, shuttered windows that evoke a sense of old-world charm, while intricate ironwork balconies add a touch of delicate artistry. The promenade itself is paved with smooth stones, inviting leisurely strolls and creating a harmonious flow along its length. Meticulously maintained gardens and lawns flank the walkway, adding a touch of natural beauty and providing a refreshing contrast to the surrounding architecture.

The combination of arcaded buildings, lush greenery, and open space creates a harmonious and inviting atmosphere. The Liston is a place where time seems to slow down, where the pace of life is leisurely, and where the beauty of the surroundings invites contemplation and relaxation.

Cultural and Social Significance

Since its construction, the Liston Promenade has been an integral part of Corfu Town's social and cultural fabric. During the 19th and early 20th centuries, the promenade was a favored gathering place for the island's aristocracy and upper classes. The arcaded buildings housed elegant cafes, restaurants, and boutiques, where the elite could enjoy coffee, engage in lively conversations, and indulge in the latest fashions.

The Liston also served as a venue for various public events and festivities, such as parades, concerts, and celebrations. The promenade's central location and spacious layout made it an ideal setting for these gatherings, fostering a sense of community and civic pride among the residents of Corfu Town.

One of the most enduring traditions associated with the Liston is the volta, a leisurely evening stroll that has been a cherished custom in Corfu for generations. Locals and visitors alike participate in this ritual, walking up and down the promenade, greeting friends and acquaintances, and enjoying the vibrant atmosphere. The volta is a reflection of the island's relaxed and sociable lifestyle, a time to connect with others, share news, and enjoy the simple pleasures of life.

Modern-Day Liston

Today, the Liston Promenade continues to be a vibrant and bustling area, attracting both locals and tourists who come to experience its unique charm and historical significance. The arcaded buildings now house a variety of cafes, restaurants, bars, and shops, offering visitors a wide range of dining, entertainment, and shopping options.

The outdoor seating areas of the cafes and restaurants are particularly popular, providing the perfect setting for enjoying a coffee, a leisurely meal, or a refreshing drink while taking in the sights and sounds of the promenade. The Liston is also a favored spot for people-watching, as the promenade is frequented by a diverse mix of residents, tourists, and street performers, creating a lively and dynamic atmosphere.

Seasonal Events and Festivities

Throughout the year, the Liston Promenade hosts a variety of seasonal events and festivities that showcase the island's rich cultural heritage and traditions. During the Easter season, the promenade becomes the focal point of Corfu's famous Easter celebrations, with processions, music, and traditional customs taking place against the backdrop of the arcaded buildings.

In the summer months, the Liston is often the site of open-air concerts, dance performances, and cultural festivals. These events bring the promenade to life with music, dance, and entertainment, creating a festive and celebratory atmosphere. The Liston's spacious layout and central location make it an ideal venue for these public gatherings, drawing large crowds of locals and visitors who come to enjoy the vibrant cultural scene.

The Christmas season transforms the Liston into a winter wonderland, with festive decorations, twinkling lights, and holiday markets adding to the charm of the promenade. The cafes and restaurants offer seasonal treats and warm beverages, providing a cozy and inviting setting for holiday celebrations.

Exploring the Surrounding Area

The Liston Promenade is ideally situated for exploring the many attractions and landmarks of Corfu Town. The Spianada, or Esplanade, is the large open square that lies adjacent to the Liston and is one of the largest squares in Greece. The Spianada is a popular spot for leisurely strolls, picnics, and outdoor activities, and it offers stunning views of the Old Fortress, which is located at the eastern end of the square.

The Old Fortress, or Palaio Frourio, is a historical landmark that dates back to the Byzantine period and was later fortified by the Venetians. Visitors can explore the fortress's ancient walls, ramparts, and buildings, and enjoy panoramic views of the town and the sea from its elevated vantage points.

The nearby Saint Michael and Saint George Palace is another significant landmark, housing the Museum of Asian Art. This neoclassical palace was built during the British protectorate and serves as a cultural and historical treasure trove, with its impressive collection of Asian art and artifacts.

Mon Repos Estate

A British Legacy

The story of Mon Repos begins in the early 19th century during the British protectorate of the Ionian Islands. Sir Frederick Adam, the British Lord High Commissioner of the Ionian Islands, envisioned a summer residence that would embody the elegance and sophistication of the era. Construction of the villa, the centerpiece of the estate, commenced in 1828 and was completed in 1831. The villa, designed by the English architect Sir George Whitmore, showcases the neoclassical architectural style that was prevalent in Europe at the time.

Sir Frederick Adam, with his deep appreciation for the island's natural beauty, played a crucial role in the development of the estate's gardens and surrounding landscape. He incorporated elements of classical European garden design, creating a harmonious blend of formal gardens, shaded groves, and open lawns that complemented the villa's elegant architecture.

From British High Commissioners to Greek Royalty

Mon Repos Estate's historical significance deepened when it transitioned from a summer residence for British High Commissioners to a royal retreat for the Greek monarchy. In 1864, the Ionian Islands were ceded to the Kingdom of Greece, and Mon Repos was gifted to King George I of Greece. The estate remained in the possession of the Greek royal family for many years, serving as a favored summer retreat where they could escape the pressures of court life and enjoy the tranquility of Corfu's natural beauty.

One of the most notable events in the estate's history occurred in 1921 when Prince Philip, Duke of Edinburgh, was born at Mon Repos. Prince Philip, the husband of Queen Elizabeth II of the United Kingdom, was born to Prince Andrew of Greece and

Denmark and Princess Alice of Battenberg. This royal connection added another layer of historical significance to Mon Repos, making it a point of interest for visitors intrigued by the intertwined histories of European royalty.

Unveiling the Past

Mon Repos Estate is not merely a place of historical significance and royal heritage; it is also a site of great archaeological importance. The estate encompasses an area rich in ancient ruins and historical remnants, offering valuable insights into Corfu's ancient past and its connections to the wider Mediterranean world.

The gardens of Mon Repos are dotted with archaeological excavations, revealing the remnants of ancient temples, baths, and other structures that date back centuries. These archaeological treasures provide a tangible link to the island's ancient civilizations and offer a glimpse into the daily lives, religious practices, and architectural achievements of the people who inhabited Corfu in ancient times.

One of the most significant archaeological sites within the estate is the Temple of Hera, dating back to the 7th century BC. The temple's ruins, discovered during excavations in the 19th and 20th centuries, provide evidence of Corfu's ancient religious practices and its connections to the wider Greek world. The remains of the temple, including columns, altars, and other architectural elements, offer a fascinating window into the island's ancient past and its role in the development of Greek religion and culture.

In addition to the Temple of Hera, the estate is home to the ruins of the Paleopolis, the ancient city of Corfu. The Paleopolis was the island's first settlement and served as its capital during the ancient and early Christian periods. The remains of the Paleopolis, including ancient walls, foundations, and artifacts, shed light on the early history of Corfu and its development as a significant urban center in the ancient world.

The Villa

The villa at Mon Repos Estate stands as a testament to the elegance and grandeur of neoclassical architecture. Its design, characterized by symmetry, proportion, and classical elements, reflects the architectural ideals of the 19th century, a period when European architecture sought to emulate the aesthetics of ancient Greece and Rome.

The villa's façade features a series of columns and pediments, creating a sense of grandeur and sophistication. The building's symmetrical design, with its balanced proportions and harmonious lines, evokes a sense of timeless beauty and architectural mastery. The interior of the villa is equally impressive, with spacious rooms, high ceilings, and large windows that allow natural light to flood the space, creating an airy and inviting atmosphere. The villa's décor includes neoclassical furnishings, artwork, and artifacts that add to its historical ambiance, offering a glimpse into the lifestyle and tastes of its former occupants.

Visitors to Mon Repos can explore the various rooms and halls of the villa, gaining a sense of the grandeur and elegance that once characterized this royal residence. The villa's historical significance, its architectural beauty, and its connection to the Greek royal family make it a captivating destination for those seeking to delve into Corfu's rich past.

The Gardens

The gardens of Mon Repos Estate are a true highlight, offering a serene and picturesque setting for visitors to enjoy. The gardens were carefully designed and landscaped, incorporating elements of classical European garden design, as well as native

Mediterranean flora. The result is a harmonious blend of formal gardens, shaded groves, and open lawns that create a tranquil and inviting atmosphere. Walking paths wind through the gardens, leading visitors to various points of interest, including ancient ruins, fountains, and statues. The gardens are home to a diverse array of plant species, including cypress trees, olive groves, and colorful flowers, creating a symphony of colors and scents that change with the seasons.

The natural beauty of the gardens, combined with the historical and archaeological significance of the estate, makes Mon Repos a unique and captivating destination. Visitors can wander through the gardens, enjoying the peaceful ambiance, exploring the ancient ruins, and appreciating the harmonious blend of nature and human artistry.

A Public Park and Cultural Venue

Today, Mon Repos Estate is a beloved public park and cultural venue, open to visitors year-round. The estate's historical and natural attractions, combined with its tranquil setting, make it a popular destination for both locals and tourists seeking a peaceful escape from the hustle and bustle of everyday life.

The gardens and walking paths provide a serene retreat where visitors can relax, explore, and connect with nature. The villa, with its museum exhibits, offers a glimpse into the estate's rich history and its royal connections. Mon Repos also hosts a variety of cultural events, performances, and exhibitions throughout the year, adding to the vibrant cultural life of Corfu. These events include concerts, art exhibitions, theatrical performances, and historical reenactments, providing visitors with a diverse range of cultural experiences.

Pristine Beaches

Glyfada Beach

Glyfada Beach, a jewel on the island of Corfu, Greece, is a haven for those seeking sun-drenched relaxation, thrilling water sports, and captivating natural beauty. Located approximately 16 kilometers west of Corfu Town, this expansive stretch of golden sand is embraced by verdant hills and the mesmerizing turquoise waters of the Ionian Sea.

Accessibility and Convenience

Reaching Glyfada Beach is a breeze, with various transportation options available. Whether you prefer the independence of a car, the convenience of a taxi, or the affordability of a bus, getting to this coastal paradise is straightforward. Ample parking areas are available near the beach, though they can fill up quickly during the peak summer months.

Beach Features and Amenities

Glyfada Beach is celebrated for its soft, golden sand that gently slopes into the crystal-clear waters, making it ideal for swimmers of all levels. Families with young children can enjoy the shallows, while experienced swimmers can venture further out to explore the deeper areas.

To enhance your comfort and enjoyment, the beach offers a range of amenities. Rent a sunbed and umbrella for a shaded retreat, or indulge in refreshments and delectable cuisine at the beach bars and restaurants lining the shore. From traditional Greek dishes to fresh seafood and international fare, there's something to satisfy every palate.

For the adventurous souls, Glyfada Beach provides an array of water sports and activities. Rent equipment for snorkeling, paddleboarding, and jet skiing, or join organized activities such as banana boat rides and parasailing. A designated beach volleyball area adds to the fun and excitement.

Lifeguards are on duty during peak season to ensure the safety of all beachgoers. Public restrooms, showers, and changing facilities are readily available, and the beach is accessible to individuals with disabilities, with ramps and pathways leading to the shore.

Natural Beauty and Scenery

Glyfada Beach is renowned for its breathtaking natural beauty. Framed by rugged cliffs and lush greenery, the beach offers a stunning backdrop for relaxation and recreation. The harmonious blend of golden sands, azure waters, and verdant hills creates a truly mesmerizing scene.

The surrounding hills and cliffs are adorned with Mediterranean vegetation, including olive trees, cypress trees, and vibrant wildflowers. These natural elements enhance the beach's charm and provide a sense of tranquility and seclusion. The cliffs also offer vantage points for capturing panoramic views of the coastline and the sea, making them a favorite spot for photographers and nature enthusiasts.

The clear waters of Glyfada Beach invite you to explore the underwater world teeming with marine life. Snorkelers can discover colorful fish, sea urchins, and various types of seaweed, while exploring the rocky formations and underwater caves.

Accommodation Options

For those who wish to stay near Glyfada Beach, a variety of accommodation options cater to different budgets and preferences.

Glyfada Beach Hotel: This beachfront hotel offers comfortable rooms with stunning sea views, direct beach access, a swimming pool, a restaurant, and a bar.

Menigos Resort: Located a short walk from the beach, Menigos Resort offers apartments and bungalows, a swimming pool, a restaurant, and a mini-market.

Corfu Glyfada Beach Apartments: These self-catering apartments are perfect for families and groups, featuring fully equipped kitchens, living areas, balconies with sea views, a swimming pool, and a garden.

Villa Glyfada: For a luxurious and private experience, Villa Glyfada offers a stunning villa with a private pool, a garden, and panoramic sea views.

Exploring the Surrounding Area
Beyond Glyfada Beach, the surrounding area offers a wealth of opportunities for exploration and adventure.

Pelekas Village: This charming village, a short drive from Glyfada Beach, is known for its traditional architecture and stunning views. Explore the narrow streets, visit local shops and tavernas, and enjoy panoramic vistas from the Kaiser's Throne viewpoint.

Myrtiotissa Beach: Considered one of Corfu's most beautiful beaches, Myrtiotissa Beach, located south of Glyfada Beach, offers a secluded and unspoiled setting with crystal-clear waters and golden sands.

Corfu Town: Corfu's capital, a UNESCO World Heritage site, boasts historical landmarks, Venetian architecture, and a vibrant atmosphere. Explore the Old Fortress, stroll along the Liston Promenade, and visit museums and galleries.

Aqualand Water Park: One of Europe's largest water parks, Aqualand, is a short drive from Glyfada Beach and offers a wide range of water slides, pools, and attractions for all ages.

Hiking and Nature Walks: The hills and countryside surrounding Glyfada Beach provide ample opportunities for hiking and nature walks, with trails leading to scenic viewpoints, ancient ruins, and traditional villages. The Corfu Trail, a long-distance hiking route, passes near Glyfada Beach and offers stunning views.

Sidari Beach and Canal d'Amour

Nestled on the northern coast of Corfu, approximately 36 kilometers from the island's capital, Sidari Beach is a vibrant and captivating destination. This expansive stretch of golden sand is not just a singular beach, but rather a diverse coastal area encompassing a series of smaller coves and bays, each possessing its own unique allure. With its shallow, crystalline waters and soft sands, Sidari Beach is a haven for families, couples, and solo travelers seeking a memorable seaside escape.

Effortless Accessibility and a Thriving Village Atmosphere

Reaching Sidari Beach is a seamless experience, thanks to the readily available transportation options. Whether you choose to travel by car, taxi, or bus, the journey is convenient and straightforward, with regular services connecting Sidari to Corfu Town and other parts of the island. Ample parking facilities near the beach ensure hassle-free arrival, while the lively village of Sidari offers a plethora of shops, restaurants, and cafes, providing all the necessities and indulgences for a comfortable and enjoyable stay.

Beach Features and Amenities

Sidari Beach is renowned for its inviting expanse of soft, golden sand and the tranquil, turquoise waters that gently lap the shore. The beach's gradual slope into the sea creates shallow areas perfect for wading and swimming, making it an ideal choice for families with young children. The clarity of the water provides exceptional visibility, making it a snorkeler's paradise, where one can observe a vibrant underwater world teeming with colorful fish and other marine life.

To enhance your beach experience, Sidari offers a comprehensive range of amenities. Comfortable sunbeds and umbrellas are available for rent, providing respite from the sun and allowing you to unwind in the shade. A variety of beach bars and restaurants line the shore, offering a tempting selection of refreshments, snacks, and meals. Savor traditional Greek dishes, fresh seafood delicacies, and international cuisine while basking in the stunning coastal vistas.

For those seeking an adrenaline rush, Sidari Beach caters to adventure enthusiasts with a variety of water sports and activities. Rent equipment for paddleboarding, jet skiing, and windsurfing, or embark on thrilling organized activities such as banana boat rides and parasailing. Designated areas for beach volleyball and other games add to the lively and dynamic atmosphere.

Ensuring the safety and comfort of all beachgoers, lifeguards are on duty during peak season. Public restrooms, showers, and changing facilities are readily available, and the beach is accessible to individuals with disabilities, with ramps and pathways leading to the shore.

Canal d'Amour

One of Sidari Beach's most iconic and distinctive features is the Canal d'Amour, also known as the Channel of Love. This captivating natural channel, carved over centuries by the relentless action of the sea on the sandstone cliffs, forms a narrow passageway extending from the beach into the sea. Encircled by dramatic rock formations, the Canal d'Amour is celebrated for its crystal-clear waters and an aura of romance that permeates the air.

Local legend claims that couples who swim through the Canal d'Amour will be blessed with eternal love and happiness. This romantic allure has made it a popular destination for couples and honeymooners, who come to immerse themselves in its enchanting beauty and make a wish for enduring love.

Beyond its romantic significance, the Canal d'Amour is also a sought-after spot for swimming and snorkeling. The exceptional water clarity provides unparalleled visibility, allowing swimmers to explore the underwater caves and fascinating rock formations. The channel's sheltered location ensures calm and gentle currents, making it suitable for swimmers of all skill levels.

For those who prefer to stay dry, the surrounding cliffs and rock formations offer captivating exploration on foot. Trails and pathways lead to vantage points that boast panoramic views of the coastline and the vast expanse of the Ionian Sea. These viewpoints are ideal for photography enthusiasts and those seeking to capture the essence of Sidari's natural beauty.

Accommodation Options

Visitors seeking accommodation near Sidari Beach and the Canal d'Amour will find a diverse range of options to suit their preferences and budgets. The area surrounding Sidari offers a mix of hotels, resorts, apartments, and villas, ensuring a comfortable and convenient stay for all.

Sidari Beach Hotel: This beachfront hotel provides comfortable rooms with breathtaking sea views, direct beach access, and amenities such as a swimming pool, restaurant, and bar.

Canal d'Amour Beachfront Apartments: Located just steps away from the Canal d'Amour, these self-catering apartments offer a convenient and comfortable stay, complete with fully equipped kitchens, living areas, and balconies with sea views.

Cavo d'Oro Complex: Situated near Sidari Beach, Cavo d'Oro Complex offers a variety of accommodation options, including apartments and studios, along with a swimming pool, restaurant, and mini-market, providing everything guests need for a relaxing stay.

Villa Kanali: For those seeking a more private and luxurious experience, Villa Kanali offers a stunning villa with a private pool, garden, and panoramic sea views. The villa's spacious and elegant design provides a perfect sanctuary for relaxation and enjoyment.

Exploring the Surrounding Area

While Sidari Beach and the Canal d'Amour are undeniably captivating, the surrounding area beckons with opportunities for exploration and adventure.

Peroulades Village: A short drive from Sidari, Peroulades is a charming village renowned for its traditional architecture and stunning vistas. Explore the labyrinthine narrow streets, browse the local shops and tavernas, and soak in the panoramic views from the famed Sunset Beach, also known as Logas Beach.

Cape Drastis: Located near Peroulades, Cape Drastis is a dramatic and picturesque cape characterized by unique rock formations and breathtaking views of the sea. Accessible by a dirt road, the cape offers a secluded and unspoiled setting for photography and exploration.

Corfu Town: No visit to Corfu is complete without experiencing Corfu Town, the island's vibrant capital. This UNESCO World Heritage site is a treasure trove of historical landmarks, Venetian architecture, and a lively atmosphere. Explore the Old Fortress, stroll along the Liston Promenade, and delve into the island's history at the numerous museums and galleries.

Acharavi: A short drive from Sidari, Acharavi is a bustling coastal town boasting a beautiful beach, a variety of shops and restaurants, and a vibrant nightlife. Enjoy water sports, explore the local markets, and savor delicious meals at traditional tavernas.

Antinioti Lagoon: Situated near the village of Agios Spyridonas, Antinioti Lagoon is a protected wetland area that offers a unique opportunity for birdwatching and nature walks. The lagoon is a haven for a variety of bird species, including herons, egrets, and kingfishers.

Agios Gordios Beach

Agios Gordios Beach, a picturesque gem on the western coast of Corfu, offers a harmonious blend of natural beauty, recreational activities, and a vibrant village atmosphere. Located approximately 16 kilometers south of Corfu Town, this expansive beach stretches for about 1.5 kilometers, providing ample space for visitors to unwind, soak up the sun, and create lasting memories. The beach's allure is further enhanced by the surrounding verdant hills, lush vegetation, and dramatic rocky formations, creating a serene and picturesque environment that captivates the senses.

Effortless Accessibility and a Welcoming Village
Reaching Agios Gordios Beach is a breeze, with convenient access by car, taxi, or bus. Regular bus services connect the beach to Corfu Town and other parts of the island, making it an easily accessible destination for those staying in various locations. While several parking areas are available near the beach, it's worth noting that they can fill up quickly during the peak summer months. The charming village of Agios Gordios, nestled near the beach, offers a delightful array of shops, restaurants, cafes, and accommodations, ensuring that visitors have everything they need for a comfortable and enjoyable stay.

Beach Features and Amenities
Agios Gordios Beach is celebrated for its soft, golden sand, which provides a striking contrast against the clear, turquoise waters of the Ionian Sea. The beach's gentle slope into the sea creates ideal conditions for swimming and wading, catering to both experienced swimmers and families with young children who can safely enjoy the shallows.

To enhance your comfort and enjoyment, the beach offers a comprehensive range of amenities. Rent a sunbed and umbrella to create a shaded oasis and unwind in comfort. Several beach bars and restaurants line the shore, offering a tempting selection of refreshments, snacks, and meals. Indulge in traditional Greek cuisine, savor fresh seafood delicacies, or explore international flavors while taking in the mesmerizing views of the sea.

For those seeking an adrenaline rush, Agios Gordios Beach provides an array of water sports and activities. Rent equipment for snorkeling, paddleboarding, and jet skiing, or embark on thrilling organized activities such as banana boat rides and parasailing. A designated beach volleyball area adds to the lively atmosphere and provides a fun way to stay active.

The safety and well-being of beachgoers are paramount, with lifeguards on duty during the peak season. Public restrooms, showers, and changing facilities are readily available, ensuring convenience for all. The beach is also accessible to individuals with disabilities, with ramps and pathways leading to the shore.

Natural Beauty and Scenery

One of the most captivating aspects of Agios Gordios Beach is its breathtaking natural beauty. Framed by rugged cliffs and lush greenery, the beach offers a stunning backdrop for relaxation and recreation. The harmonious blend of golden sands, azure waters, and verdant hills creates a truly mesmerizing scene.

The surrounding hills and cliffs are adorned with a rich variety of Mediterranean vegetation, including olive trees, cypress trees, and vibrant wildflowers. These natural elements enhance the beach's charm and provide a sense of tranquility and seclusion. The cliffs also offer vantage points that boast panoramic views of the coastline and the vast expanse of the Ionian Sea, making them a favorite spot for photographers and nature enthusiasts.

The crystal-clear waters of Agios Gordios Beach beckon you to explore the underwater world teeming with marine life. Snorkelers can discover colorful fish, sea urchins, and various types of seaweed, while exploring the fascinating rock formations and underwater caves.

Accommodation Options

Visitors seeking accommodation near Agios Gordios Beach will find a diverse range of options to suit their preferences and budgets. The area surrounding the beach offers a mix of hotels, resorts, apartments, and villas, ensuring a comfortable and convenient stay for all.

Agios Gordios Beach Hotel: This beachfront hotel provides comfortable rooms with breathtaking sea views, direct beach access, and amenities such as a swimming pool, restaurant, and bar.

Mayor La Grotta Verde Grand Resort: Nestled on a hillside overlooking Agios Gordios Beach, this 5-star resort offers luxurious accommodations with breathtaking views of the sea. The resort features elegant rooms and suites, multiple restaurants, a spa, and a range of recreational activities.

Sebastian's Family Hotel: A charming family-run hotel situated in the heart of Agios Gordios village, offering cozy rooms and apartments, a restaurant serving delicious Greek cuisine, and a friendly, welcoming atmosphere.

Dina's Paradise Apartments: These self-catering apartments are ideal for families and groups, complete with fully equipped kitchens, living areas, and balconies with sea views. The complex also features a swimming pool and garden.

Villa Sophia: For those seeking a more private and luxurious experience, Villa Sophia offers a stunning villa with a private pool, garden, and panoramic sea views. The villa's spacious and elegant design provides a perfect sanctuary for relaxation and enjoyment.

Exploring the Surrounding Area

While Agios Gordios Beach is undeniably captivating, the surrounding area beckons with opportunities for exploration and adventure.

Pelekas Village: A short drive from Agios Gordios, Pelekas is a charming village renowned for its traditional architecture and stunning vistas. Explore the labyrinthine narrow streets, browse the local shops and tavernas, and soak in the panoramic views from the famed Kaiser's Throne viewpoint.

Myrtiotissa Beach: Located just north of Agios Gordios, Myrtiotissa Beach is often hailed as one of Corfu's most beautiful beaches. This secluded and unspoiled haven boasts crystal-clear waters and golden sands, making it an ideal spot for swimming and sunbathing.

Corfu Town: No visit to Corfu is complete without experiencing Corfu Town, the island's vibrant capital. This UNESCO World Heritage site is a treasure trove of historical landmarks, Venetian architecture, and a lively atmosphere. Explore the Old Fortress, stroll along the Liston Promenade, and delve into the island's history at the numerous museums and galleries.

Aqualand Water Park: A short drive from Agios Gordios Beach, Aqualand is one of Europe's largest water parks, offering a thrilling day out for families and adventure seekers. With a wide range of water slides, pools, and attractions for all ages, Aqualand promises a day of fun and excitement.

Hiking and Nature Walks: The hills and countryside surrounding Agios Gordios Beach provide ample opportunities for hiking and nature walks. Explore the numerous trails that lead to scenic viewpoints, ancient ruins, and traditional villages. The Corfu Trail, a long-distance hiking route, passes near Agios Gordios Beach and offers stunning views of the coastline and interior.

Outdoor Activities

Snorkeling and Diving Spots

Corfu's Underwater Wonders

Corfu, with its captivating coastline and crystal-clear waters, offers a wealth of opportunities for underwater exploration. From vibrant coral reefs to intriguing underwater caves, the island's diverse marine life and fascinating underwater landscapes beckon snorkelers and divers alike.

Paleokastritsa

Often hailed as one of Corfu's premier snorkeling and diving destinations, Paleokastritsa is a picturesque village nestled on the western coast of the island. Surrounded by lush hills and dotted with stunning beaches and coves, Paleokastritsa offers an idyllic setting for underwater adventures.

Snorkeling

The shallow waters near Paleokastritsa's beaches provide ideal conditions for snorkeling, with calm waters and exceptional visibility. Popular snorkeling spots include:

Agios Spyridon Beach: This expansive beach offers ample space for snorkelers to explore the vibrant underwater world. Colorful fish, sea urchins, and even the occasional octopus can be spotted in these clear waters.

Ampelaki Beach: This secluded cove offers a more intimate snorkeling experience, with calm waters and a diverse array of marine life.

Alipa Beach: This picturesque beach is known for its rocky seabed and underwater caves, providing an exciting environment for snorkelers to discover hidden treasures.

Diving

For those seeking deeper underwater adventures, Paleokastritsa offers exceptional diving sites, including the renowned Blue Caves.

Blue Caves: These mesmerizing underwater caves and tunnels are adorned with vibrant corals and sponges, creating a surreal and captivating underwater landscape. Divers can encounter a variety of marine life, including groupers, moray eels, and even barracudas.

Reefs and Walls: Paleokastritsa's reefs and walls provide thrilling diving experiences, with depths ranging from 10 to 40 meters. Divers can explore these underwater formations and encounter a diverse array of marine creatures.

Agni Bay

Located on the northeastern coast of Corfu, Agni Bay is another fantastic destination for snorkeling and diving. This tranquil bay is known for its crystal-clear waters and serene atmosphere, providing an ideal setting for underwater exploration.

Snorkeling

The calm and clear waters of Agni Bay are perfect for snorkelers of all levels. The bay is home to a variety of marine life, including colorful fish, sea urchins, and starfish. The rocky seabed and underwater vegetation create a picturesque underwater environment, where snorkelers can easily spot schools of fish swimming among the rocks and seaweed.

Diving

Agni Bay offers excellent diving opportunities for both beginners and experienced divers. The bay features several dive sites with varying depths and underwater landscapes.

Agni Reef: This beautiful underwater reef teems with marine life, including vibrant corals, sponges, and sea fans. Divers can encounter species such as groupers, octopuses, and nudibranchs.

Clear Visibility and Calm Conditions: Agni Bay's clear visibility and calm conditions make it an ideal spot for underwater photography and exploration.

Kassiopi

Kassiopi, a charming fishing village on the northeastern coast of Corfu, is renowned for its beautiful beaches and crystal-clear waters. The underwater world of Kassiopi is equally impressive, offering a diverse array of marine life and intriguing underwater landscapes.

Snorkeling

The rocky coastline and clear waters of Kassiopi make it a great destination for snorkeling. Popular snorkeling spots include:

Bataria Beach: This picturesque beach offers calm waters and excellent visibility, making it easy to spot colorful fish, sea urchins, and starfish.

Kanoni Beach: This secluded cove offers a more intimate snorkeling experience, with a diverse array of marine life to discover.

Diving

Kassiopi offers several exciting dive sites, including underwater caves, reefs, and walls.

Kassiopi Caves: These underwater caves and tunnels are adorned with corals and sponges, creating a fascinating environment for exploration. Divers can encounter marine life such as moray eels, groupers, and octopuses.

Reefs: The nearby reefs provide excellent diving opportunities, with depths ranging from 10 to 30 meters. Divers can explore these vibrant ecosystems and encounter a variety of marine creatures.

Nissaki

Nissaki, a quaint village on the northeastern coast of Corfu, is known for its crystal-clear waters and serene atmosphere. The underwater world of Nissaki is rich in marine life and offers excellent snorkeling and diving experiences.

Snorkeling

The shallow waters near Nissaki Beach are perfect for snorkeling. The beach is sheltered by rocky outcrops, creating calm and clear waters ideal for underwater exploration. Snorkelers can observe a variety of marine life, including colorful fish, sea urchins, and starfish. The rocky seabed and underwater vegetation add to the beauty of the underwater environment.

Diving

Nissaki offers several excellent dive sites, including underwater reefs and walls.

Nissaki Reef: This popular diving spot is known for its vibrant corals and sponges. Divers can explore the reef's diverse marine life, including groupers, moray eels, and octopuses.

Clear Visibility and Calm Conditions: Nissaki's clear visibility and calm conditions make it an ideal destination for underwater photography and exploration.

Ermones

Ermones, located on the western coast of Corfu, is a picturesque bay surrounded by lush green hills. The clear waters and diverse marine life make Ermones a fantastic destination for snorkeling and diving.

Snorkeling

The shallow waters near Ermones Beach are ideal for snorkeling. The rocky seabed and underwater caves provide an exciting environment for underwater exploration. Snorkelers can observe a variety of marine life, including colorful fish, sea urchins, and starfish. The clear visibility and calm conditions make Ermones an excellent spot for snorkeling.

Diving

Ermones offers several exceptional dive sites, including underwater reefs and walls.

Ermones Reef: This popular diving spot is known for its vibrant corals and sponges. Divers can explore the reef's diverse marine life, including groupers, moray eels, and octopuses.

Walls: The nearby walls offer thrilling diving experiences, with depths ranging from 10 to 30 meters. Divers can explore these underwater formations and encounter a variety of marine creatures.

Kalami

Kalami, a charming village on the northeastern coast of Corfu, is known for its beautiful beaches and crystal-clear waters. The underwater world of Kalami is equally impressive, with a diverse array of marine life and intriguing underwater landscapes.

Snorkeling

The clear and calm waters of Kalami Bay are perfect for snorkeling. The bay is home to a variety of marine life, including colorful fish, sea urchins, and starfish. The rocky seabed and underwater vegetation create a picturesque underwater environment. Snorkelers can easily spot schools of fish swimming around the rocks and seaweed.

Diving

Kalami offers several exciting dive sites, including underwater caves, reefs, and walls.

Kalami Caves: These underwater caves and tunnels are adorned with corals and sponges, creating a fascinating environment for exploration. Divers can encounter marine life such as moray eels, groupers, and octopuses.

Reefs: The nearby reefs provide excellent diving opportunities, with depths ranging from 10 to 30 meters. Divers can explore these vibrant ecosystems and encounter a variety of marine creatures.

Kavos

Kavos, located on the southern coast of Corfu, is known for its lively atmosphere and vibrant nightlife. However, the underwater world of Kavos is equally captivating, with excellent snorkeling and diving opportunities.

Snorkeling

The clear and calm waters near Kavos Beach are perfect for snorkeling. The beach is sheltered by rocky outcrops, creating an ideal environment for underwater exploration. Snorkelers can observe a variety of marine life, including colorful fish, sea urchins, and starfish. The rocky seabed and underwater vegetation add to the beauty of the underwater environment.

Diving

Kavos offers several excellent dive sites, including underwater reefs and walls.

Kavos Reef: This popular diving spot is known for its vibrant corals and sponges. Divers can explore the reef's diverse marine life, including groupers, moray eels, and octopuses.

Clear Visibility and Calm Conditions: Kavos' clear visibility and calm conditions make it an ideal destination for underwater photography and exploration.

Agios Gordios

Agios Gordios, located on the western coast of Corfu, is one of the island's most picturesque and beloved beaches. The underwater world of Agios Gordios is just as captivating, with a rich diversity of marine life and fascinating rock formations.

Snorkeling

The shallow waters near Agios Gordios Beach are perfect for snorkeling. The beach is surrounded by rocky cliffs, creating an exciting environment for underwater exploration. Snorkelers can observe a variety of marine life, including colorful fish, sea urchins, and starfish. The clear visibility and calm conditions make Agios Gordios an excellent spot for snorkeling.

Diving

Agios Gordios offers several exceptional dive sites, including underwater reefs and walls.

Agios Gordios Reef: This popular diving spot is known for its vibrant corals and sponges. Divers can explore the reef's diverse marine life, including groupers, moray eels, and octopuses.

Walls: The nearby walls offer thrilling diving experiences, with depths ranging from 10 to 30 meters. Divers can explore these underwater formations and encounter a variety of marine creatures.

Boat Rentals and Tours

Boat Rentals

Renting a boat in Corfu empowers you to explore the island's hidden gems, secluded beaches, and charming coves at your leisure. Several companies and rental agencies offer a diverse range of boats, from small motorboats to luxurious yachts, ensuring that there's a perfect vessel for every type of adventurer.

Types of Boat Rentals

Small Motorboats: Ideal for beginners and those without a boating license, small motorboats are easy to operate and perfect for exploring the coastline. These boats typically accommodate up to 6 people and come equipped with essential safety gear and navigation equipment. Renting a small motorboat allows you to visit nearby beaches, coves, and islands, enjoying the freedom of the open sea.

Speedboats: For those seeking a more exhilarating experience, speedboats offer increased power and speed, allowing you to cover greater distances in less time. Speedboats are ideal for exploring multiple destinations in a single day, participating in water sports, and enjoying the thrill of riding the waves.

Sailing Yachts: Sailing yachts provide a more leisurely and traditional boating experience, harnessing the power of the wind to propel you across the water. These boats are perfect for those who appreciate the art of sailing and wish to experience Corfu's beauty from a different perspective.

Luxury Yachts: For those seeking the ultimate in comfort and indulgence, renting a luxury yacht is the epitome of opulence. These vessels come equipped with top-of-the-line amenities, including spacious cabins, lounges, kitchens, and even jacuzzis. Luxury yachts are ideal for special occasions, private events, and extended trips, offering a lavish and unforgettable experience.

Popular Boat Rental Locations

Gouvia Marina: One of the largest marinas in the Ionian Sea, Gouvia Marina is a popular hub for boat rentals. The marina offers a wide range of boats for rent, as well as excellent facilities, including shops, restaurants, and fueling stations. Located just a few kilometers from Corfu Town, Gouvia Marina is easily accessible and provides convenient access to the island's northern and eastern coasts.

Paleokastritsa: Renowned for its stunning beaches and crystal-clear waters, Paleokastritsa is another popular location for boat rentals. Several rental agencies operate in the area, offering motorboats, speedboats, and yachts for rent. Paleokastritsa's beautiful bays, coves, and underwater caves make it an ideal destination for boating enthusiasts.

Kassiopi: This charming fishing village on the northeastern coast of Corfu is a great place to rent a boat and explore the surrounding waters. Kassiopi's picturesque harbor is home to several rental agencies, providing a range of boats for hire. The nearby coves, beaches, and rocky outcrops offer plenty of opportunities for exploration.

Requirements and Safety

Renting a boat in Corfu is generally a straightforward process, but there are a few requirements and safety considerations to keep in mind:

No License Required: For small motorboats with engines up to 30 horsepower, no boating license is required. These boats are easy to operate, and rental agencies provide a brief orientation and safety instructions before departure.

License Required: For speedboats, sailing yachts, and larger boats, a valid boating license is required. If you don't have a license, many rental agencies offer the option to hire a skipper who can operate the boat for you.

Safety Gear: All rental boats come equipped with essential safety gear, including life jackets, first aid kits, and navigation equipment. It's crucial to familiarize yourself with the safety procedures and equipment before setting out.

Weather Conditions: Always check the weather forecast before heading out on the water. Avoid boating in adverse weather conditions, and be aware of any changes in the weather during your trip.

Organized Boat Tours

For those who prefer a guided experience, organized boat tours offer a fantastic way to explore Corfu's coastline and nearby islands. Several tour operators provide a variety of boat tours, each with its own unique itinerary and highlights.

Types of Boat Tours

Sightseeing Tours: Sightseeing boat tours are designed to showcase the best of Corfu's natural beauty and historical landmarks. These tours often include visits to iconic spots such as the Old Fortress, the Liston Promenade, and the Achilleion Palace. Passengers can enjoy panoramic views of the coastline, learn about the island's history from knowledgeable guides, and take in the stunning scenery.

Beach Hopping Tours: Beach hopping tours are perfect for those who want to visit multiple beaches in one day. These tours typically include stops at some of Corfu's most beautiful and secluded beaches, such as Glyfada Beach, Myrtiotissa Beach, and Agios Gordios Beach. Passengers can swim, snorkel, and relax on the sandy shores, enjoying the crystal-clear waters and picturesque surroundings.

Sunset Cruises: Sunset cruises offer a romantic and serene way to experience Corfu's coastline. These tours usually depart in the late afternoon and sail along the coast as the sun sets over the Ionian Sea. Passengers can enjoy stunning views of the sunset, sip on cocktails, and savor the tranquil atmosphere. Some sunset cruises also include dinner or appetizers on board.

Snorkeling and Diving Tours: For underwater enthusiasts, snorkeling and diving tours provide an opportunity to explore Corfu's vibrant marine life and underwater landscapes. These tours typically include stops at popular snorkeling and diving spots, such as Paleokastritsa, Agni Bay, and Nissaki. Passengers can swim, snorkel, and dive in the clear waters, discovering colorful fish, corals, and underwater caves.

Island Hopping Tours: Island hopping tours offer the chance to visit some of the nearby islands and islets, such as Paxos and Antipaxos, known for their stunning beaches and crystal-clear waters. These tours often include stops at picturesque harbors, charming villages, and secluded coves, allowing passengers to explore the unique beauty of each island.

Popular Boat Tour Operators

Paxos and Antipaxos Cruises: Several operators offer day trips to the islands of Paxos and Antipaxos. These tours typically depart from Corfu Town or Gaios and include stops at beautiful beaches, sea caves, and the charming village of Gaios. Passengers can swim, snorkel, and explore the unique landscapes of these nearby islands.

Blue Caves and Sivota Cruises: Departing from Corfu Town or Kassiopi, these tours take passengers to the famous Blue Caves and the coastal village of Sivota. The Blue Caves are known for their stunning turquoise waters and intricate rock formations, while Sivota offers picturesque harbors and lovely beaches. Passengers can explore the caves, swim in the clear waters, and enjoy the scenic beauty of Sivota.

Glass-Bottom Boat Tours: Glass-bottom boat tours provide a unique way to experience Corfu's underwater world without getting wet. These tours typically depart from Paleokastritsa or Corfu Town and offer panoramic views of the seabed through the glass-bottom panels. Passengers can observe marine life, underwater caves, and coral formations while learning about the marine ecosystem from knowledgeable guides.

Private Boat Tours: For a more personalized experience, several operators offer private boat tours that can be customized to suit your preferences. Private tours allow you to create your own itinerary, visit specific destinations, and enjoy a more intimate and exclusive experience.

Horseback Riding and Adventure Sports

Popular Horseback Riding Locations

Trail Riding in the Countryside: Corfu's interior boasts a network of trails that wind through picturesque landscapes, making it an ideal destination for trail riding. Riders can traverse through olive groves, vineyards, and forests, experiencing the island's natural beauty up close. These trails often lead to breathtaking viewpoints, where riders can pause to admire panoramic vistas of the countryside and the glistening Ionian Sea.

Beach Riding: One of the most enchanting experiences Corfu offers is horseback riding along its pristine beaches. Imagine the sensation of riding on golden sands, with the gentle waves lapping at the shore and the refreshing sea breeze caressing your face. Beach rides are typically conducted during the early morning or late afternoon to avoid the midday heat and ensure a peaceful and enjoyable experience.

Riding Through Traditional Villages: Horseback riding tours often incorporate visits to traditional Corfiot villages, providing a glimpse into the island's rich cultural heritage. Riders can explore narrow streets, admire traditional architecture, and interact with friendly locals, gaining a deeper appreciation for Corfu's authentic charm.

Notable Equestrian Centers

Trailriders Corfu: Located in Avlaki, Trailriders Corfu is a well-established equestrian center offering a variety of horseback riding tours. Their experienced guides lead riders through scenic trails in the countryside, olive groves, and along the coastline. Trailriders Corfu caters to riders of all levels, providing well-trained horses and all necessary equipment.

Silvaland Equestrian Center: Situated in Ano Korakiana, Silvaland Equestrian Center is another popular choice for horseback riding enthusiasts. The center offers a range of riding tours, including trail rides through the countryside and beach rides along the coast. Silvaland also provides riding lessons for beginners and advanced riders, as well as pony rides for children.

Saddle Up Ranch: Located in Kato Korakiana, Saddle Up Ranch offers guided horseback riding tours through the lush landscapes of northern Corfu. Riders can explore scenic trails, traditional villages, and olive groves, all while enjoying the companionship of well-trained horses.

Adventure Sports

For those seeking an adrenaline rush, Corfu offers a diverse range of adventure sports catering to all levels of thrill-seekers. From water sports to land-based activities, the island's varied landscapes provide the perfect backdrop for an exciting and adventurous experience.

Popular Adventure Sports

Water Sports: The crystal-clear waters of the Ionian Sea are perfect for a variety of water sports, including jet skiing, windsurfing, kitesurfing, paddleboarding, and parasailing. Several beaches across the island offer equipment rentals and lessons for these activities, making it easy for visitors to dive into the action.

Scuba Diving and Snorkeling: Corfu's underwater world is teeming with marine life and fascinating rock formations. Scuba diving and snorkeling are popular activities that allow adventurers to explore vibrant reefs, underwater caves, and even shipwrecks. Dive centers across the island offer guided dives and courses for beginners and experienced divers.

Rock Climbing and Canyoning: The rugged cliffs and gorges of Corfu provide excellent opportunities for rock climbing and canyoning. Climbers can scale challenging rock faces and enjoy breathtaking views from the top. Canyoning involves descending narrow gorges and waterfalls, navigating through natural rock formations and pools. Experienced guides and safety equipment are essential for these activities.

Mountain Biking: Corfu's diverse terrain offers a variety of trails for mountain biking enthusiasts. Riders can explore scenic routes through olive groves, forests, and traditional villages, enjoying the thrill of off-road cycling. Mountain bike rentals and guided tours are available across the island.

Hiking and Trekking: For those who prefer exploring on foot, Corfu offers numerous hiking and trekking trails that traverse the island's picturesque landscapes. Popular routes include the Corfu Trail, a long-distance path that covers approximately 220 kilometers and passes through diverse terrains, including coastal paths, mountainous regions, and traditional villages. Guided hikes and trekking tours are available for those who want to discover the island's hidden gems.

Notable Adventure Sports Providers

Corfu Sea School: Located in Gouvia Marina, Corfu Sea School offers a range of water sports activities, including sailing, windsurfing, and paddleboarding. The school provides equipment rentals, lessons, and guided tours, catering to all skill levels.

Corfu Scuba Diving: This dive center, located in Paleokastritsa, offers scuba diving courses and guided dives at some of the best dive sites in Corfu. Their experienced instructors ensure a safe and enjoyable diving experience, whether you're a beginner or an advanced diver.

Explore The Outside: Based in Paleokastritsa, Explore The Outside offers a variety of adventure sports activities, including rock climbing, canyoning, hiking, and mountain biking. Their experienced guides provide all necessary equipment and ensure a safe and thrilling experience for participants.

Corfu Mountain Biking: This company offers guided mountain biking tours that explore the scenic trails and landscapes of Corfu. They provide high-quality mountain bikes, safety gear, and expert guides to ensure an enjoyable and adventurous ride.

Dining and Nightlife

Best Seafood Restaurants

Toula's Seaside

Nestled in the tranquil embrace of Agni Bay on Corfu's northeastern coast, Toula's Seaside is a renowned waterfront restaurant that has been delighting diners since 1981. This family-run establishment exudes a laid-back atmosphere, inviting guests to relax and savor the stunning views of the turquoise sea while indulging in fresh, flavorful seafood. Toula's Seaside specializes in Mediterranean-inspired dishes, showcasing the bounty of the sea with expertly prepared catches.

Avli

In the heart of Corfu Town, Avli restaurant offers a delightful escape from the bustling city streets. With its cozy ambiance and friendly staff, Avli provides a welcoming haven where you can savor the freshest seafood delicacies while soaking in the vibrant atmosphere of the town. The restaurant's menu features a tempting array of seafood dishes, including grilled fish, calamari, and seafood pasta, all prepared with the finest ingredients and a touch of Mediterranean flair.

Anthos Restaurant

Located near the historic Old Fortress in Corfu Town, Anthos Restaurant is a popular destination for seafood aficionados. Renowned for its fresh and flavorful dishes, the restaurant offers a wide range of seafood options, including grilled octopus, seafood risotto, and fish souvlaki. The cozy and welcoming atmosphere makes it an ideal spot for a romantic dinner or a memorable gathering with family and friends.

Psaraki

In the charming village of Benitses, Psaraki is a family-run taverna that captures the essence of traditional Corfiot cuisine. This authentic eatery specializes in fresh seafood dishes, showcasing the island's rich culinary heritage. The menu features a variety of local catches, including grilled fish, seafood stews, and fried calamari, all prepared with time-honored recipes and a passion for authentic flavors.

Mare Azzurro Cafe Restaurant

Located in the scenic village of Agios Gordios, Mare Azzurro Cafe Restaurant offers a delightful dining experience with breathtaking views of the Ionian Sea. The restaurant's menu features a wide selection of seafood dishes, including grilled sea bass, seafood pasta, and fresh oysters. The relaxed and inviting atmosphere makes it a perfect spot for a leisurely meal by the sea, where you can savor the flavors of the Mediterranean while enjoying the gentle sea breeze and stunning coastal vistas.

Taverna Kalami

Situated right on the beach in Kalami, Taverna Kalami is a popular destination for seafood lovers seeking a beachfront dining experience. The restaurant's menu features a variety of fresh catches, including grilled fish, seafood salads, and traditional Greek seafood stews. With its beautiful beachfront location and friendly staff, Taverna Kalami offers an idyllic setting to savor the flavors of the sea while enjoying the soothing sounds of the waves.

Aristos Taverna Kaliviotis

Located in the village of Kaliviotis, Aristos Taverna Kaliviotis is known for its exceptional seafood dishes and warm hospitality. The restaurant's menu features a variety of fresh catches, including grilled octopus, seafood pasta, and fish souvlaki. The cozy and inviting atmosphere makes it a perfect spot for a memorable dining experience, where you can savor delicious seafood while enjoying the genuine warmth and hospitality of the staff.

The Three Brothers

Situated in the village of Agios Spyridon, The Three Brothers is a popular taverna specializing in fresh seafood dishes. The restaurant's menu features a variety of grilled fish, seafood stews, and traditional Greek seafood delicacies. With its friendly staff and charming ambiance, The Three Brothers is a must-visit for seafood enthusiasts seeking an authentic Corfiot dining experience.

Manthos Restaurant-Bar

Located in the village of Agios Georgios Pagon, Manthos Restaurant-Bar offers a delightful dining experience with stunning views of the Ionian Sea. The restaurant's menu features a wide selection of fresh seafood dishes, including grilled fish, seafood pasta, and fresh oysters. The relaxed and inviting atmosphere makes it a perfect spot for a memorable meal by the sea, where you can savor the flavors of the Mediterranean while enjoying the breathtaking coastal scenery.

Taverna Sunrise

Situated in the village of Agios Stefanos, Taverna Sunrise is a popular spot for seafood lovers seeking a beachfront dining experience. The restaurant's menu features a variety of fresh catches, including grilled fish, seafood salads, and traditional Greek seafood stews. With its beautiful beachfront location and friendly service, Taverna Sunrise is an excellent choice for a seaside dining experience, where you can savor the flavors of the sea while enjoying the gentle sea breeze and stunning coastal vistas.

Local Bars and Clubs

Bristol Cafe

Located in the heart of Corfu Town, Bristol Cafe is a beloved establishment that seamlessly transitions from a chic cafe by day to a lively bar by night. With its stylish decor and welcoming atmosphere, Bristol Cafe is a favorite among locals and tourists alike. During the day, it's the perfect spot to relax with a coffee or an early evening drink, while as the night progresses, the bar transforms into a vibrant hub with great music and a fantastic selection of cocktails. The outdoor seating area provides a charming setting to soak in the beauty of Corfu Town's old streets while enjoying a refreshing beverage.

Tartaya Tiki Bar

For a unique and exotic experience, Tartaya Tiki Bar on Corfu Town's bustling Disco Strip offers a delightful blend of Tiki and Corfiot vibes. With its Hawaiian-inspired decor and a spacious outdoor area adorned with palm trees, Tartaya Tiki Bar creates a fun and relaxed atmosphere that transports you to a tropical paradise. The bar is renowned for its creative cocktails, expertly crafted by skilled mixologists, and the friendly staff ensures a welcoming and enjoyable experience.

EDEM Beach Club

Situated on the shoreline of Dassia Beach, EDEM Beach Club is a celebrated venue for those seeking a vibrant nightlife experience with a beachfront twist. The club offers a lively atmosphere with pulsating music, refreshing cocktails, and convenient beachside services. Visitors can dance the night away under the stars while enjoying stunning views of the Ionian Sea. EDEM Beach Club is open every night, making it a perfect destination for a fun and unforgettable night out.

54 Dreamy Nights Club

Located in the commercial heart of Corfu Town, 54 Dreamy Nights Club is the island's largest and most lavish nightclub. This upscale venue boasts impressive lighting and sound equipment, creating a luxurious and modern atmosphere that sets the stage for an electrifying night. The club features renowned DJs spinning a mix of hip-hop, deep house, and Greek music, catering to a diverse range of musical tastes. 54 Dreamy Nights Club also hosts events and concerts by professional artists, adding to its vibrant and dynamic nightlife scene.

Yard Club

Yard Club, situated in Corfu Town, is a popular nightclub known for its chic and friendly atmosphere. The club offers a great selection of drinks and hosts special events on different weekdays, catering to a variety of musical preferences. On Wednesdays, Yard Club organizes parties featuring music from Athens, while Fridays are dedicated to electronic tunes, and Saturdays to RnB nights. The club's welcoming environment and diverse music selection make it an ideal spot for a night of dancing and socializing.

The Boathouse Bar & Cocktails

Nestled on the seafront in Roda, The Boathouse Bar & Cocktails offers fantastic views of Albania and a relaxed seaside atmosphere. The bar is known for its extensive selection of cocktails, expertly crafted by skilled bartenders, and the friendly staff ensures a welcoming and enjoyable experience. It's a perfect spot to unwind after a day of exploring Corfu's beautiful beaches and landscapes, enjoying a refreshing drink while soaking in the tranquil seaside ambiance.

The Vine

Located in Corfu Town, The Vine is a popular wine bar that exudes a sophisticated yet approachable vibe. The bar offers an impressive selection of wines from around the world, catering to connoisseurs and casual drinkers alike. In addition to its extensive wine list, The Vine also serves a variety of cocktails and soft drinks, making it a great spot to enjoy a night out with friends. The cozy ambiance and welcoming atmosphere make The Vine a favorite among locals and tourists.

Maria's Famous Karaoke Fun Pub

For a night of laughter and entertainment, Maria's Famous Karaoke Fun Pub in Corfu Town is the place to be. This lively venue offers a fun and entertaining atmosphere, where visitors can showcase their singing talents and enjoy a night of karaoke. With its friendly staff and vibrant ambiance, Maria's Famous Karaoke Fun Pub is a great spot to let loose, have fun, and create unforgettable memories.

The Lemon Tree

Located in Agios Gordios, The Lemon Tree is a popular bar known for its fantastic atmosphere and expertly crafted cocktails. The bar offers a cozy and inviting environment, making it a perfect spot to relax and enjoy a drink with friends. The friendly staff and lively ambiance make The Lemon Tree a favorite among visitors seeking a casual and enjoyable night out.

Vintage Cocktail Bar

Situated at the beginning of the Disco Strip in Corfu Town, Vintage Cocktail Bar is a stylish venue known for its amazing cocktails and welcoming atmosphere. The bar offers a great selection of classic and contemporary cocktails, expertly prepared by skilled mixologists. The chic decor and lively ambiance make Vintage Cocktail Bar a perfect spot for a sophisticated night out.

Gourmet Experiences

Fine Dining Restaurants

Corfu boasts a collection of fine dining restaurants that elevate the island's culinary scene to new heights. These establishments showcase the finest local ingredients, innovative culinary techniques, and exquisite presentations, creating a symphony of flavors that will delight even the most discerning palates.

Venetian Well: Located in the heart of Corfu Town, Venetian Well is a charming fine dining restaurant that exudes elegance and sophistication. Housed in a beautifully restored building, the restaurant offers a romantic ambiance and a menu that celebrates Mediterranean and Greek cuisine. Diners can savor exquisite dishes such as grilled octopus, seafood risotto, and lamb tenderloin, expertly paired with a curated selection of local and international wines.

Pomo D'Oro: Pomo D'Oro is a modern gourmet restaurant situated in Corfu Town, known for its creative approach to Mediterranean cuisine. The restaurant's menu features a harmonious blend of flavors, with dishes inspired by the rich culinary traditions of Greece and Italy. Guests can indulge in culinary delights such as truffle pasta, seared scallops, and slow-cooked beef cheeks, all beautifully presented and bursting with flavor. The contemporary decor and attentive service make Pomo D'Oro a top choice for a sophisticated dining experience.

The White House Restaurant: Set in the idyllic village of Kalami, The White House Restaurant offers a unique dining experience with stunning views of the Ionian Sea. This family-run restaurant, situated in the historic Durrell family's residence, serves a menu that pays homage to Corfiot and Mediterranean cuisine. Diners can enjoy dishes such as fresh seafood platters, grilled fish, and traditional Greek meze while taking in the breathtaking coastal scenery. The warm hospitality and serene atmosphere make The White House Restaurant a must-visit for food enthusiasts.

Salto Wine Bar and Bistro: Located in the heart of Corfu Town, Salto Wine Bar and Bistro is a chic dining spot that offers a contemporary take on Greek and Mediterranean cuisine. The menu features a variety of gourmet dishes, including grilled prawns, lamb shank, and wild mushroom risotto, each thoughtfully paired with an extensive selection of wines from Greece and beyond. The stylish decor and vibrant ambiance create the perfect setting for a memorable dining experience.

Culinary Tours and Workshops

For those seeking a deeper understanding of Corfu's culinary heritage, a variety of culinary tours and workshops offer immersive experiences that will tantalize your taste buds and expand your knowledge of the island's gastronomic traditions.

Corfu Gastronomy Tour: Embark on a culinary adventure with the Corfu Gastronomy Tour, an immersive experience that takes you on a journey through the island's rich food culture. Led by knowledgeable local guides, the tour includes visits to traditional markets, artisan food shops, and family-run tavernas. Participants can sample a variety of local specialties, including olive oil, cheese, honey, and wine, while learning about the island's culinary traditions and history. The tour also includes hands-on cooking demonstrations and opportunities to interact with local producers and chefs.

Olive Oil Tasting and Tour: Olive oil is an integral part of Corfiot cuisine, and the Olive Oil Tasting and Tour offers a fascinating insight into the production and flavors of this essential ingredient. Participants visit a traditional olive oil mill, where they learn about the olive harvesting and pressing process. The tour includes a guided tasting of different olive oil varieties, allowing participants to discover the nuances of flavor, aroma, and texture. The experience is complemented by a visit to an olive grove, where participants can learn about the cultivation and care of olive trees.

Wine Tasting and Vineyard Tour: Corfu's vineyards produce a variety of excellent wines, and the Wine Tasting and Vineyard Tour provides an opportunity to explore the island's winemaking heritage. Participants visit local wineries and vineyards, where they learn about the grape varieties, winemaking techniques, and terroir that contribute to the unique character of Corfiot wines. The tour includes guided tastings of red, white, and rosé wines, accompanied by expert commentary and food pairings. Some tours also offer the chance to meet the winemakers and tour the cellars and production facilities.

Cooking Classes and Workshops: For those who wish to delve deeper into the culinary arts, Corfu offers a range of cooking classes and workshops that provide hands-on instruction in traditional and contemporary Greek cuisine. Participants can learn to prepare a variety of dishes, from classic Greek meze and moussaka to modern seafood creations and gourmet desserts. The classes are led by experienced chefs and home cooks who share their knowledge, techniques, and passion for Corfiot cuisine. Some workshops also include visits to local markets to source fresh ingredients and gain insight into the island's food culture.

Herbal Walks and Foraging Tours: Corfu's diverse landscape is home to a wealth of wild herbs and edible plants that have been used in the island's cuisine for centuries. Herbal walks and foraging tours offer a unique opportunity to explore the natural beauty of Corfu while learning about its rich botanical heritage. Led by knowledgeable guides, participants embark on guided walks through forests, fields, and coastal areas, where they identify and gather wild herbs, flowers, and greens. The tours often include discussions on the culinary and medicinal uses of the plants, as well as demonstrations on how to incorporate them into traditional recipes.

Gourmet Events and Festivals

Corfu's vibrant culinary scene is celebrated through various gourmet events and festivals that showcase the island's local produce, culinary traditions, and festive spirit.

Corfu Food and Wine Festival: The Corfu Food and Wine Festival is an annual event that celebrates the island's vibrant culinary scene and local produce. Held in various locations across Corfu Town, the festival features a series of food and wine tastings, cooking demonstrations, workshops, and cultural performances. Visitors can sample a diverse array of dishes prepared by local chefs, discover new wines from Corfiot vineyards, and participate in interactive cooking classes. The festival also showcases traditional music and dance, creating a lively and festive atmosphere.

Easter Celebrations: Easter is a significant event in Corfu, marked by elaborate celebrations and a rich culinary tradition. The island's Easter festivities include processions, concerts, and the famous Pot Throwing tradition, where locals hurl clay pots from their balconies to mark the Resurrection. The culinary highlights of Easter include traditional dishes such as tsoureki (sweet bread), magiritsa (Easter soup), and lamb on the spit. Visitors can experience the island's unique Easter customs and savor the delicious flavors of the festive season.

Harvest Festivals: Corfu's agricultural heritage is celebrated through various harvest festivals that take place throughout the year. These events highlight the island's local produce, including olives, grapes, honey, and citrus fruits. Harvest festivals often include traditional music and dance, food tastings, and cooking demonstrations. Visitors can learn about the island's farming traditions, sample fresh and seasonal dishes, and participate in activities such as grape stomping and olive picking.

Unique Dining Experiences

Corfu offers a range of unique dining experiences that go beyond the traditional restaurant setting, creating unforgettable memories and immersing you in the island's culinary culture.

Dinner on a Boat: For a truly unforgettable dining experience, consider booking a dinner on a boat. Several companies in Corfu offer private boat charters that include a gourmet meal prepared by a personal chef. Guests can enjoy a leisurely cruise along the island's coastline, taking in the stunning views and savoring a delicious multi-course dinner. The menu typically features fresh seafood, local specialties, and fine wines, creating a magical and romantic setting for a special occasion.

Farm-to-Table Dining: Farm-to-table dining experiences are gaining popularity in Corfu, offering guests the opportunity to enjoy meals made from fresh, locally sourced ingredients. Several restaurants and farms across the island provide farm-to-table dining experiences, where guests can tour the farm, meet the producers, and enjoy a meal prepared from the day's harvest. These experiences highlight the island's commitment to sustainable and seasonal cuisine, allowing guests to connect with the land and the people behind their food.

Picnic in the Vineyards: For a relaxed and intimate dining experience, consider booking a picnic in the vineyards. Several wineries in Corfu offer picnic packages that include a selection of local cheeses, charcuterie, fresh bread, and wine. Guests can enjoy their picnic amidst the scenic vineyards, taking in the beautiful surroundings and savoring the flavors of Corfu. This unique dining experience provides a peaceful and idyllic setting for a leisurely meal.

Shopping and Souvenirs

Fashion and Accessories

High-End Boutiques and Designer Stores
For those seeking luxury and sophistication, Corfu boasts a selection of high-end boutiques and designer stores that showcase the latest trends and timeless classics.

Velvet Corfu: Located in Corfu Town, Velvet Corfu is a chic boutique that offers a curated selection of international and Greek designer brands. The store features a range of stylish clothing, accessories, and jewelry, perfect for those who appreciate high-quality fashion. From elegant dresses and sophisticated handbags to trendy shoes and chic jewelry, Velvet Corfu has something for every fashion lover.

Muses Corfu: Muses Corfu is a concept store that goes beyond fashion, offering a unique shopping experience that blends tradition, culture, contemporary art, and design. The store showcases exceptional Greek collections, with a focus on sustainable and eco-friendly products. Muses Corfu features a variety of clothing, accessories, and home decor items that reflect the island's rich heritage and modern sensibilities.

Concept Store Corfu: Concept Store Corfu is another must-visit destination for fashion enthusiasts. The store offers a wide range of contemporary and traditional Greek fashion, including dresses, casual wear, resort wear, and accessories. With its eclectic mix of styles and emphasis on quality, Concept Store Corfu is the perfect place to find unique and stylish pieces that express your individuality.

Traditional Markets and Local Shops

Corfu's traditional markets and local shops offer a glimpse into the island's authentic charm and provide an opportunity to discover unique treasures.

Corfu Central Market: The Corfu Central Market is a bustling hub of activity, offering a wide variety of fresh produce, local delicacies, and handmade items. Located in the heart of Corfu Town, the market is a sensory feast, with vibrant colors, enticing aromas, and a lively atmosphere. It's a great place to explore and discover unique fashion and accessory finds, from handmade jewelry and traditional textiles to locally crafted bags and scarves.

Old Town Corfu: The Old Town of Corfu is a charming area filled with narrow alleyways, historic buildings, and quaint shops. Shopping in the Old Town is a delightful experience, as you can wander through the labyrinthine streets and browse through local boutiques, artisanal shops, and souvenir stores. The area is known for its unique items, such as traditional Greek jewelry, handcrafted accessories, and locally made clothing. The blend of history, culture, and shopping makes the Old Town a must-visit destination.

Local Designers and Artisans

Corfu is home to a talented community of local designers and artisans who create exquisite pieces that reflect the island's rich heritage and artistic spirit.

Panos Zinas: Panos Zinas is an internationally recognized Greek designer known for his luxury accessories and ready-to-wear collections. His designs are characterized by high style, top-quality fabrics, and a keen eye for timeless chic. Panos Zinas has dressed well-known local and international women, including singers, actresses, and models. His collections feature luxurious gowns, cocktail dresses, and beachwear that are perfect for any fashion enthusiast.

Aggeliki Tasopoulou: Aggeliki Tasopoulou is a talented designer specializing in evening dresses and wedding gowns. Her designs are known for their elegance, sophistication, and meticulous attention to detail. With a focus on high-quality fabrics and skilled craftsmanship, Aggeliki Tasopoulou creates stunning pieces that are perfect for special occasions.

Ifigenia Loukou: Ifigenia Loukou is a rising star in the world of jewelry design. Her creations are inspired by Greek mythology, nature, and contemporary art, resulting in unique and exquisite pieces. Ifigenia Loukou's jewelry is perfect for those who appreciate intricate craftsmanship and artistic expression. Her collections feature a variety of necklaces, bracelets, earrings, and rings that make a statement and add a touch of elegance to any outfit.

Must-Have Items

When shopping in Corfu, there are certain must-have items that capture the essence of the island and make for perfect souvenirs or gifts.

Kumquat Products: Kumquats are a specialty of Corfu, and the island offers a variety of products made from this unique citrus fruit. From jams and marmalades to liquors and cosmetics, kumquat products are a delightful way to savor the flavors of Corfu.

Handmade Jewelry: Corfu is home to many talented artisans who create beautiful handmade jewelry. From traditional Greek designs to modern, contemporary pieces, there is a wide range of options to choose from. Handmade jewelry adds a personal touch to any outfit and makes for a thoughtful gift.

Traditional Textiles: Corfu's rich textile heritage is reflected in the traditional fabrics and garments available on the island. Items such as woven fabrics, embroidered linens, and handcrafted bags are perfect for adding a touch of Greek culture to your wardrobe or home decor.

Local Ceramics and Pottery: Corfu's pottery and ceramics are known for their intricate designs and vibrant colors. From decorative plates and bowls to unique vases and figurines, local ceramics make for beautiful and authentic souvenirs or home decor items.

Local Art and Craft Shops

Ceramic Art and Pottery Shops

Corfu has a long and rich tradition of ceramic art, with skilled artisans crafting beautiful and functional pieces that reflect the island's cultural heritage.

Keramikart - Ceramic Workshop: Located in the picturesque village of Pelekas, Keramikart is a renowned ceramic workshop and gallery that offers a delightful collection of handcrafted pottery. The workshop is run by a talented team of artisans who create a variety of ceramic items, including decorative plates, bowls, vases, and figurines. Each piece is meticulously crafted and hand-painted, reflecting the traditional techniques and vibrant colors of Corfiot ceramics. Visitors can also participate in pottery workshops and learn the art of ceramics from skilled craftsmen, gaining a deeper appreciation for this ancient craft.

Corfu Ceramics: Situated in the heart of Corfu Town, Corfu Ceramics is a charming shop that specializes in traditional and contemporary ceramic art. The shop features a wide range of ceramic items, from intricately designed tableware and home decor to unique art pieces and souvenirs. The vibrant colors and intricate patterns of the ceramics capture the beauty and spirit of Corfu, making them perfect keepsakes and gifts.

Siora Rosa Ceramic Studio: Located in the village of Arillas, Siora Rosa Ceramic Studio is a family-run workshop that creates stunning handmade ceramics inspired by the natural beauty of Corfu. The studio offers a variety of ceramic items, including decorative plates, bowls, tiles, and sculptures. Each piece is crafted with great attention to detail, using traditional techniques and natural materials. Visitors to the studio can watch the artisans at work, gaining insight into the creative process, and even try their hand at pottery, creating their own unique piece to take home.

Jewelry and Accessories Shops

Corfu's jewelry and accessories shops offer a dazzling array of handcrafted pieces that reflect the island's rich cultural heritage and artistic flair.

Ifigenia Jewelry: Ifigenia Jewelry, situated in Corfu Town, is a boutique that offers exquisite handmade jewelry inspired by Greek mythology, nature, and contemporary art. The shop features a variety of necklaces, bracelets, earrings, and rings, each meticulously crafted with fine materials and intricate designs. Ifigenia's creations are perfect for those who appreciate unique and artistic jewelry that makes a statement.

Artemis Art and Jewelry: Located in the Old Town of Corfu, Artemis Art and Jewelry is a delightful shop that offers a diverse collection of handcrafted jewelry and accessories. The shop features pieces made from a variety of materials, including silver, gold, gemstones, and natural elements. The designs range from traditional Greek motifs to modern and minimalist styles, ensuring there is something for every taste and preference.

Gekko Workshop: Gekko Workshop, situated in the village of Kassiopi, is a small artisan shop that specializes in handmade jewelry and accessories. The workshop offers a variety of unique pieces, including bracelets, necklaces, and earrings made from natural stones, seashells, and recycled materials. The designs are inspired by the beauty of Corfu's landscapes and the island's vibrant culture, making them perfect mementos of your visit.

Art Galleries and Studios

Corfu's art galleries and studios provide a platform for local and international artists to showcase their creativity and offer visitors a glimpse into the island's vibrant art scene.

Corfu Gallery: Located in Corfu Town, Corfu Gallery is a contemporary art space that showcases the works of local and international artists. The gallery features a diverse collection of paintings, sculptures, and mixed-media pieces that reflect the rich cultural heritage and modern influences of Corfu. The gallery also hosts regular exhibitions, art events, and workshops, providing a platform for artists to connect with the community and share their creative vision.

Kyma Fine Art: Kyma Fine Art, situated in the charming village of San Stefanos, is an art gallery and studio that offers a curated selection of contemporary artworks. The gallery features pieces by established and emerging artists, including paintings, photography, and sculptures. Kyma Fine Art is dedicated to promoting the local art scene and supporting the creative community, making it a must-visit destination for art enthusiasts.

Angel's Art Gallery: Located in the village of Dassia, Angel's Art Gallery is a family-run gallery that showcases a beautiful collection of paintings, ceramics, and handcrafted items. The gallery features works by local artists, each capturing the essence of Corfu's landscapes, culture, and traditions. Visitors can browse through the diverse collection and find unique pieces that make for perfect souvenirs and gifts.

Handicrafts and Souvenirs

Corfu offers a variety of traditional handicrafts and souvenirs that capture the essence of the island's culture and heritage.

Komboloi - Greek Worry Beads: Komboloi, or Greek worry beads, are a traditional accessory that has been part of Greek culture for centuries. Several shops in Corfu specialize in handmade komboloi, offering a variety of designs and materials, including amber, wood, and semi-precious stones. These beautiful and tactile items are perfect keepsakes and gifts that carry a piece of Greek tradition.

Corfiot Lace and Embroidery: Corfu is known for its intricate lace and embroidery, which have been crafted by local artisans for generations. Several shops across the island offer a variety of handmade lace and embroidered items, including tablecloths, napkins, and decorative linens. These exquisite pieces are crafted with great attention to detail and make for elegant and timeless souvenirs.

Olive Wood Crafts: Olive wood crafts are a popular and sustainable souvenir from Corfu. Several shops and workshops on the island offer a variety of handcrafted olive wood items, including kitchen utensils, bowls, cutting boards, and decorative pieces. The natural beauty and durability of olive wood make these items perfect for practical use and home decor.

Traditional Markets and Art Fairs

Corfu's traditional markets and art fairs offer a vibrant and immersive shopping experience, where you can discover unique treasures and connect with local artisans.

Corfu Central Market: The Corfu Central Market, located in Corfu Town, is a vibrant and bustling hub where visitors can find a wide variety of local products and handmade items. The market offers fresh produce, local delicacies, and unique crafts, making it a great place to explore and discover Corfiot art and culture.

Traditional Village Markets: Several villages across Corfu host traditional markets where local artisans and producers sell their handmade crafts and products. These markets offer a more intimate and authentic shopping experience, allowing visitors to interact with the artisans and learn about their craft.

Art Fairs and Festivals: Corfu hosts several art fairs and festivals throughout the year, providing a platform for local artists and craftsmen to showcase their work. These events offer a unique opportunity to explore a diverse range of art and crafts, from paintings and sculptures to jewelry and textiles.

Specialty Food Stores

Traditional Delicacies and Local Produce

Kumquat Products: The kumquat, a small citrus fruit with a sweet and tangy flavor, is a symbol of Corfu's culinary identity. This versatile fruit is used to create a variety of products, including liqueurs, marmalades, sweets, and preserves. Local producers like Mavromatis Kumquat and Lazaris Distillery & Artisan Sweets are renowned for their high-quality kumquat products, crafted using traditional recipes and methods that preserve the fruit's unique flavor.

Olive Oil and Olives: Olive oil is the cornerstone of Corfiot cuisine, and the island's olive groves produce some of the finest extra virgin olive oils in the world. Specialty stores and local markets offer a wide range of olive oil products, including flavored oils, organic options, and artisanal blends. In addition to olive oil, these stores often carry a selection of olives, such as Kalamata olives, green olives, and stuffed olives, providing a taste of the Mediterranean. The Governor Olive Mill and Corfu Olive Wood are notable destinations for olive oil connoisseurs.

Honey and Beekeeping Products: Corfu's honey is renowned for its rich flavor and natural purity, a testament to the island's diverse flora and the dedication of local beekeepers. Specialty food stores offer a variety of honey products, including thyme honey, forest honey, and flower honey, each with its own distinct flavor profile. In addition to honey, these stores often carry other beekeeping products, such as bee pollen, propolis, and beeswax, known for their health benefits and natural properties. Melissokomiki Corfu and Vasilakis Estate are popular destinations for high-quality honey and beekeeping products.

Cheese and Dairy Products: Corfu's cheese and dairy products are an integral part of the island's culinary heritage, reflecting the island's agricultural traditions and the art of cheesemaking. Specialty stores offer a variety of traditional cheeses, such as feta, graviera, and manouri, as well as unique local varieties like Corfiot ladotyri, a cheese preserved in olive oil. These cheeses are often made from sheep's or goat's milk and are known for their rich flavors and artisanal quality. Corfu Cheese Shop and Dairy Farm Vasiliou are excellent places to find a wide selection of local cheeses and dairy products.

Artisanal Products and Gourmet Treats

Corfu's artisanal producers and confectioners create a delightful array of gourmet treats that will satisfy even the most discerning sweet tooth.

Baklava and Pastries: Baklava, a sweet pastry made from layers of filo dough, nuts, and honey, is a beloved treat in Corfu and throughout Greece. Specialty stores and bakeries across the island offer a variety of baklava and other traditional Greek pastries, such as kataifi, loukoumades, and galaktoboureko. These delicacies are made using time-honored recipes and high-quality ingredients, ensuring a delicious and authentic taste. Papagiorgis Bakery and Serano Patisserie are renowned for their exceptional pastries.

Spices and Herbs: Spices and herbs play a crucial role in Greek cuisine, adding depth and complexity to a variety of dishes. Specialty food stores in Corfu offer a wide range of spices and herbs, including oregano, thyme, rosemary, sage, and mint, all essential ingredients in traditional Corfiot cooking. These stores often carry blends and mixes, such as tzatziki seasoning, souvlaki spice, and Greek herb blends, making it easy to recreate authentic flavors at home. Spices & Herbs Corfu and The Spice Shop are popular destinations for high-quality spices and herbs.

Artisan Breads and Bakery Goods: Corfu is home to several artisanal bakeries that produce a variety of traditional breads and bakery goods, using high-quality ingredients and time-honored baking methods. From rustic sourdough loaves and sesame-coated koulouri to sweet tsoureki and melomakarona, there is a wide range of baked goods to enjoy. Lemoni Bakery and Fournoi Kassianos are well-known for their exceptional bakery products.

Gourmet Chocolate and Confections: For those with a sweet tooth, Corfu offers a variety of specialty stores that produce gourmet chocolates and confections. These stores create exquisite treats using high-quality ingredients and artisanal techniques, resulting in a symphony of flavors and textures. From rich chocolate truffles and handmade pralines to candied fruits and nougat, there is a delightful array of sweets to choose from. Corfu Chocolaterie and Sweet Corner are popular destinations for gourmet chocolates and confections.

Wine and Spirits

Corfu's vineyards and distilleries produce a variety of exceptional wines and spirits that reflect the island's unique terroir and traditional methods.

Local Wineries: Corfu's wine production has a long and storied history, with several local wineries producing high-quality wines that express the island's unique character. Specialty wine stores and wineries offer a wide range of local wines, including red, white, and rosé varieties. Visitors can sample wines made from indigenous grape varieties, such as Kakotrygis and Skopelitiko, as well as international varieties. Notable wineries include Theotoky Estate and Grammenos Winery.

Kumquat Liqueur: Kumquat liqueur is a signature product of Corfu, made from the island's beloved kumquat fruit. The liqueur is known for its bright orange color and distinctive sweet and tangy flavor, making it a popular souvenir and a delightful addition to cocktails and desserts. Several distilleries and specialty stores produce and sell kumquat liqueur, often offering tastings and tours. Lazaris Distillery & Artisan Sweets and Mavromatis Kumquat are well-known producers of high-quality kumquat liqueur.

Tsipouro and Ouzo: Tsipouro and ouzo are traditional Greek spirits that are deeply ingrained in Corfu's culture. Tsipouro is a strong distilled spirit made from grape pomace, while ouzo is an anise-flavored liqueur. Specialty stores and local distilleries offer a variety of tsipouro and ouzo, often produced using traditional methods and recipes, preserving the authentic flavors of these iconic Greek spirits. Corfu Distillery and Ouzeri Tsitsanis are excellent places to find a selection of these traditional drinks.

Specialty Markets and Food Halls

Corfu's specialty markets and food halls offer a vibrant and immersive shopping experience, where you can discover a diverse range of local and artisanal products.

Corfu Central Market: The Corfu Central Market, located in Corfu Town, is a bustling hub where visitors can find a wide variety of fresh produce, local delicacies, and specialty food items. The market offers an array of products, including fresh fruits and vegetables, seafood, meats, cheeses, olives, and herbs. It is an excellent place to explore and discover the flavors of Corfu, with vendors offering tastings and samples of their products.

Gastronomy Hall: Gastronomy Hall is a specialty food market in Corfu Town that brings together a diverse selection of local and artisanal products. The market features stalls and shops offering a variety of gourmet items, including cheeses, cured meats, olive oils, honey, spices, and pastries. Gastronomy Hall is a great destination for food lovers looking to sample and purchase high-quality Corfiot products.

Organic Markets: Corfu is home to several organic markets that offer a range of organic and sustainably produced food items. These markets feature products such as organic fruits and vegetables, free-range eggs, artisanal breads, and natural cosmetics. Green Market and Eco Market are popular destinations for those seeking organic and eco-friendly products.

Local Festivals and Events

Easter Celebrations

Easter in Corfu is an extraordinary event that transcends the typical religious holiday. It's a vibrant and deeply cherished celebration, considered one of the most magnificent and unique in all of Greece. The island transforms into a living canvas of religious rituals, cultural traditions, and joyous festivities, captivating both locals and visitors alike. The atmosphere is infused with a sense of reverence, joy, and community spirit, creating an unforgettable experience for all who participate.

Preparing for the Holy Week

The anticipation for Easter in Corfu begins weeks in advance, as locals engage in various customs and traditions to prepare for the Holy Week. Homes are meticulously cleaned and adorned with festive decorations, symbolizing renewal and purity. Traditional Easter foods, such as tsoureki (sweet bread) and koulourakia (butter cookies), are lovingly prepared, filling homes with enticing aromas. The community comes together for spiritual gatherings and cultural events, fostering a sense of unity and anticipation for the upcoming celebrations.

Holy Week

Holy Week, or Megali Evdomada, marks the pinnacle of the Easter celebrations in Corfu. Each day of this sacred week is observed with unique rituals and events that reflect the island's deep-rooted Orthodox Christian faith and cultural heritage.

Palm Sunday: The week commences with Palm Sunday, commemorating Jesus' triumphant entry into Jerusalem. The faithful gather in churches for services, where palm leaves are blessed and distributed to the congregation. These palm leaves are then carried home and used to adorn homes and streets, symbolizing victory and peace.

Holy Monday to Holy Wednesday: These days are dedicated to introspection and prayer, with special services held in churches across the island. The Gospels are read, and hymns are chanted, recounting the events leading up to Jesus' crucifixion. The atmosphere is one of solemnity and reflection as individuals prepare themselves spiritually for the culmination of Holy Week.

Holy Thursday: This day holds profound significance, marked by the reenactment of the Last Supper and the Washing of the Feet, symbolizing humility and service. In the evening, a somber service known as the Service of the Twelve Gospels is held, during which twelve Gospel readings recount the Passion of Christ. The service concludes with the Crucifixion Procession, where an effigy of Christ on the cross is carried through the streets, accompanied by mournful hymns and the tolling of church bells.

Good Friday: Good Friday, or Megali Paraskevi, is the most solemn day of Holy Week, commemorating the crucifixion and death of Jesus. The day begins with the Service of the Royal Hours, a series of prayers and hymns that reflect on the suffering of Christ. In the afternoon, the Descent from the Cross service takes place, during which the body of Christ is symbolically removed from the cross and placed in the Epitaphios, a beautifully decorated bier representing Christ's tomb.

One of the most poignant and visually striking events of Good Friday is the Epitaphios Procession. Each church on the island has its own Epitaphios, and these biers are carried through the streets by parishioners, accompanied by choirs singing mournful hymns and bands playing dirges. The processions from different churches often converge in the central squares, creating a powerful and moving spectacle of faith and communal solidarity.

Holy Saturday: Holy Saturday, or Megalo Savato, marks a transition from mourning to anticipation of the resurrection. In the morning, a unique and exuberant tradition takes place in Corfu Town: the Pot Throwing ceremony. At 11:00 AM sharp, residents throw clay pots filled with water from their balconies, shattering them on the streets below. This custom, believed to have Venetian origins, symbolizes the renewal of life and the casting away of the old. The streets erupt with the sound of crashing pottery and the laughter of spectators, creating a joyful and chaotic scene.

As night falls on Holy Saturday, the atmosphere shifts to one of anticipation and reverence. The faithful gather in churches and the main square for the Resurrection Service, which begins around 11:00 PM. The service is filled with the chanting of hymns and the reading of the Gospel that recounts the resurrection of Christ. At midnight, the lights are extinguished, and the Holy Flame is brought out by the priest, symbolizing the resurrection of Jesus. The flame is passed from candle to candle among the congregation, illuminating the night with a warm, golden glow.

The moment of resurrection is marked by the joyous proclamation Christos Anesti (Christ is Risen), to which the congregation responds Alithos Anesti (Truly He is Risen). Fireworks illuminate the sky, church bells ring out, and the air is filled with celebration and jubilation. The faithful then carry the holy flame back to their homes, where they use it to light their lamps and candles, symbolizing the light of the resurrection entering their lives.

Easter Sunday: Easter Sunday, or Kyriaki tou Pascha, is a day of pure festivity and celebration. Families gather for a grand Easter feast, sharing a variety of traditional dishes, such as magiritsa (a lamb offal soup), roasted lamb, and tsoureki (a sweet braided bread). The table is adorned with red-dyed eggs, symbolizing the blood of Christ and the promise of new life. The tradition of egg tapping takes place, where individuals tap their eggs against each other, with the one whose egg remains uncracked declared the winner.

The joyous spirit of Easter Sunday continues throughout the day, with music, dancing, and socializing filling the streets and squares. Local communities organize various events and activities, including folk dances, live performances, and games, ensuring that everyone partakes in the celebration.

Easter Monday: Easter Monday, or Deutera tou Pascha, is an extension of the festive spirit, with families and friends continuing their gatherings and celebrations. Picnics in the countryside and visits to monasteries and churches are common, offering prayers of thanksgiving and seeking blessings for the year ahead.

Corfu Carnival

The Corfu Carnival, affectionately known as Apokries, is an explosion of vibrant energy and joyous celebration that engulfs the entire island. This captivating event, deeply rooted in ancient Greek traditions and infused with Venetian and Italian influences, is a spectacle of colorful parades, elaborate costumes, lively music, and infectious merriment. Taking place in the weeks leading up to Lent, the carnival culminates in a grand finale on Clean Monday, leaving a lasting impression on all who witness its magic.

Preparing for the Festivities

The anticipation for the Corfu Carnival begins weeks in advance, as communities and organizations across the island come together to meticulously plan and organize the various events. Corfu Town and surrounding villages are adorned with vibrant decorations, transforming the island into a festive wonderland. The excitement builds with each passing day, culminating in the official kickoff on Tsiknopempti, or Smoky Thursday. This day is dedicated to feasting on grilled meats, and the air is filled with the tantalizing aroma of barbecued delicacies. Locals gather with friends and family to share a festive meal, marking the beginning of the carnival season.

A Kaleidoscope of Events and Traditions

The Corfu Carnival is a whirlwind of events and activities that bring the spirit of celebration to every corner of the island. One of the highlights is the Petegoletsa, or Gossip, a traditional street theater performance that unfolds in the heart of the Old Town. Performers, clad in elaborate costumes, reenact humorous and satirical skits, playfully poking fun at local characters and events. The audience, often joining in the witty banter, fills the streets with laughter and applause, creating a lively and interactive spectacle.

The centerpiece of the Corfu Carnival is undoubtedly the grand parade, a spectacular procession that winds its way through the streets of Corfu Town. Participants don imaginative costumes, ranging from historical and mythological figures to contemporary characters and satirical representations. The parade features a dazzling array of floats, each meticulously designed and decorated to reflect the year's chosen theme. Accompanied by marching bands, dancers, and performers, the floats create a mesmerizing spectacle of color and movement. Spectators line the streets, cheering and clapping as the parade passes by, fully immersed in the joyous spirit of the carnival.

Children hold a special place in the Corfu Carnival, and several events are dedicated to their enjoyment. The children's parade is a delightful procession where young participants, dressed in colorful costumes, take to the streets with boundless energy and enthusiasm. Their laughter and dancing, their painted faces and sparkling eyes, add a heartwarming touch to the festivities. In addition to the parade, various games, competitions, and workshops are organized for children, ensuring that the youngest revelers have a memorable and fun-filled experience.

Music, Merriment, and Mock Weddings

Music is the heartbeat of the Corfu Carnival, and the island's rich musical heritage is showcased through numerous performances and concerts. Traditional Ionian bands, known for their distinctive brass and woodwind instruments, fill the air with lively tunes that inspire spontaneous dancing and singing. Concerts featuring local musicians and choirs are held in various venues, providing a diverse range of musical experiences for attendees. From traditional folk songs to contemporary hits, the music of the Corfu Carnival creates an infectious energy that permeates the festivities.

One of the most anticipated events of the Corfu Carnival is the Corfiot Wedding, a humorous reenactment of a traditional Corfiot wedding ceremony. This lively performance features participants dressed as the bride, groom, and wedding party, complete with exaggerated costumes and makeup. The mock wedding procession, accompanied by music and dancing, parades through the streets, much to the delight of onlookers. The bride and groom exchange humorous vows, and the ceremony is often filled with playful antics and witty commentary, showcasing the island's love for humor and theatricality.

The Grand Finale

As the Corfu Carnival reaches its climax, the grand finale, known as the Karnavalos, takes place. This spectacular event is a culmination of weeks of celebration and features a stunning display of floats, costumes, and performances. The highlight of the finale is the burning of the King Carnival, a large effigy symbolizing the end of the carnival season and the beginning of Lent. The effigy is paraded through the streets before being set ablaze in a dramatic and symbolic ceremony. The sight of the burning effigy, accompanied by fireworks and music, creates a powerful and memorable conclusion to the carnival festivities.

A Feast for the Senses

Throughout the Corfu Carnival, local cuisine plays a central role in the celebrations. Food stalls and vendors line the streets, offering a delectable array of traditional treats and festive delicacies. From savory dishes such as souvlaki, loukaniko (Greek sausage), and spanakopita (spinach pie) to sweet delights like loukoumades (honey-drenched doughnuts) and baklava, there is no shortage of delicious options to satisfy every palate. The communal aspect of sharing food and drinks with friends and family enhances the sense of camaraderie and joy that defines the carnival.

A Celebration of History and Culture

The Corfu Carnival is not merely a celebration of fun and revelry; it is also deeply rooted in the island's history and cultural heritage. The traditions and customs observed during the carnival reflect the rich tapestry of influences that have shaped Corfu over the centuries. From ancient Greek rituals to Venetian and Italian influences, the Corfu Carnival is a testament to the island's ability to blend diverse cultural elements into a harmonious and vibrant celebration.

An Inclusive and Unforgettable Experience

For visitors to Corfu, the carnival offers a unique opportunity to immerse themselves in the island's culture and experience the warmth and hospitality of its people. The inclusive nature of the celebrations ensures that everyone, regardless of age or background, can join in the festivities and create lasting memories. Whether participating in the grand parade, enjoying a street performance, or savoring a delicious treat, the Corfu Carnival provides an unforgettable and enriching experience for all.

As the carnival season draws to a close and the island transitions into the more contemplative period of Lent, the memories of the vibrant celebrations linger in the hearts of those who took part. The Corfu Carnival, with its unique blend of tradition, humor, music, and joy, leaves a lasting impression, creating a sense of anticipation for the next year's festivities. For the people of Corfu, the carnival is a cherished tradition that brings the community together in a shared celebration of life, culture, and the enduring spirit of the island.

Music and Dance Festivals

Corfu, an island steeped in cultural heritage and a deep-rooted passion for the arts, pulsates with a vibrant rhythm of music and dance festivals throughout the year. These festivals, a testament to the island's artistic spirit, bring together local and international talent, creating an enchanting symphony of sounds and movements that captivate both residents and visitors. From the grandeur of classical concerts in historic venues to the infectious energy of traditional dance performances in picturesque villages, Corfu's festivals offer a diverse and captivating cultural experience.

Corfu International Festival

The Corfu International Festival stands as a beacon of cultural prominence, drawing artists and audiences from around the globe. Held annually in Corfu Town, this prestigious festival showcases a diverse program of music, dance, theater, and visual arts, transforming the island into a hub of creative expression.

Historic theaters, open-air stages, and picturesque squares serve as enchanting venues for the festival's performances, creating an atmosphere of grandeur and intimacy. Renowned for its high artistic standards, the Corfu International Festival is committed to showcasing both established and emerging talent, offering a platform for artistic innovation and cultural exchange.

From soul-stirring classical concerts and graceful ballet performances to avant-garde contemporary dance and thought-provoking experimental theater, the festival's program caters to a wide range of artistic tastes. It's a celebration of creativity, diversity, and the transformative power of the arts.

Corfu Philharmonic Society

The Corfu Philharmonic Society, established in the early 19th century, is a cornerstone of the island's musical heritage. This esteemed institution has nurtured generations of musicians and continues to enrich the island's cultural landscape with its numerous concerts and events.

The Corfu Philharmonic Festival, a highlight of the society's calendar, features performances by its various ensembles, including orchestras, bands, and choirs. Guest artists from Greece and abroad also grace the stage, adding to the festival's international flair.

The repertoire is a delightful blend of classical masterpieces, traditional Greek melodies, contemporary compositions, and popular genres, catering to a diverse audience. The Corfu Philharmonic Festival is a testament to the island's enduring musical legacy and its commitment to fostering musical talent.

Ionian Music Academy Festival

The Ionian Music Academy Festival, organized by the Ionian University, is a vibrant platform for students, faculty, and guest artists to showcase their musical prowess and collaborate on innovative projects. The festival's program is a melting pot of musical styles and genres, ranging from classical and jazz to electronic and world music.

Concerts, masterclasses, workshops, and lectures provide opportunities for learning, collaboration, and artistic growth. Young musicians benefit from the guidance of renowned artists and educators, fostering a spirit of mentorship and creative exchange. The Ionian Music Academy Festival is a testament to the island's commitment to nurturing the next generation of musicians and promoting musical diversity.

Corfu Jazz World Music Festival

The Corfu Jazz World Music Festival is a celebration of global musical traditions, bringing together jazz and world music artists for a series of captivating concerts and jam sessions. Held in various venues across the island, the festival features a diverse lineup of local and international musicians, creating an eclectic and vibrant atmosphere.

From the soulful melodies of traditional jazz and blues to the infectious rhythms of Afrobeat, Latin, and fusion music, the festival's program is a journey through the world's musical landscape. The relaxed and friendly atmosphere encourages spontaneous collaborations and interactions between artists and audiences, fostering a sense of community and shared appreciation for music.

Celebrating Tradition

Traditional Greek music and dance are deeply ingrained in Corfu's cultural identity, and the island hosts several festivals that honor these art forms.

The Corfu Folklore Festival, held in various villages across the island, is a vibrant celebration of traditional Greek music, dance, and customs. Local folk dance groups, musicians, and singers come together to showcase the island's rich cultural heritage, adorned in traditional costumes and playing traditional instruments. The festival is a joyous expression of Corfu's cultural pride and a testament to the enduring power of tradition.

The Varkarola Festival, held in the picturesque village of Paleokastritsa, is a unique and enchanting event that commemorates the miracle of Saint Spyridon, the patron saint of Corfu. The festival's highlight is a spectacular boat parade, featuring beautifully decorated boats illuminated by lanterns and torches, sailing through the bay accompanied by traditional music and hymns. The procession culminates in a grand fireworks display, painting the night sky with vibrant colors and creating a magical atmosphere.

Carnival, Classical Music, Rock, and Dance

The Corfu Carnival, or Apokries, is another lively and colorful celebration that infuses music and dance into its festivities. The carnival, taking place in the weeks leading up to Lent, features parades, street performances, and parties, with participants dressed in elaborate costumes and masks. Bands, DJs, and musicians perform at various venues, creating a festive and energetic atmosphere.

For classical music enthusiasts, the Corfu Summer Music Festival offers a series of concerts and performances held in some of the island's most beautiful and historic venues. Renowned soloists, chamber ensembles, and orchestras grace the stage, presenting a diverse repertoire that spans from Baroque and Classical to Romantic and contemporary works.

The Corfu Rock Festival caters to rock and alternative music fans, bringing together local and international bands and artists for a series of high-energy concerts. The festival's lively atmosphere and diverse lineup create a sense of community and shared passion for music.

The Corfu Dance Festival is a celebration of dance in all its forms, featuring performances by local and international dance companies, workshops, and masterclasses. The festival's program encompasses a wide range of dance styles, from classical ballet and contemporary dance to traditional Greek dances and modern street dance, showcasing the versatility and artistry of this expressive art form.

7 Days Itinerary

Day 1: Arrival and Exploration of Corfu Town

Morning: Arrive at Corfu International Airport Ioannis Kapodistrias (CFU) and transfer to your chosen accommodation in Corfu Town. Take some time to settle in, unpack, and freshen up after your journey.

Late Morning: Embark on a leisurely stroll through the enchanting Corfu Old Town, a UNESCO World Heritage site. Lose yourself in the labyrinthine cobblestone streets, admiring the Venetian architecture, historic buildings, and charming squares. Make your way to the Liston Promenade, a beautiful arcaded walkway lined with cafes and restaurants, and enjoy a coffee or refreshing drink while soaking in the vibrant atmosphere.

Afternoon: Immerse yourself in Corfu's history by visiting its iconic landmarks. Explore the Old Fortress (Palaio Frourio), a massive Venetian fortress that offers panoramic views of the town and the sparkling sea. Stroll along the Esplanade (Spianada), the largest square in Greece, and visit the nearby Saint Michael and Saint George Palace, which houses the Museum of Asian Art. Enjoy a leisurely lunch at a traditional taverna in the Old Town, savoring authentic Greek dishes and fresh seafood.

Evening: Indulge in a gourmet dining experience at a fine dining restaurant, such as Venetian Well or Etrusco, where you can savor exquisite Mediterranean cuisine. After dinner, immerse yourself in Corfu Town's vibrant nightlife. Explore the local bars and clubs, such as La Grotta Lounge & Pub or Fuego Beach Bar, and enjoy live music, dancing, and expertly crafted cocktails.

Day 2: Beaches and Coastal Beauty

Morning: After a leisurely breakfast, head to Glyfada Beach, one of the most renowned and picturesque beaches on the island. Spend the morning swimming in the crystal-clear turquoise waters, sunbathing on the golden sands, and enjoying water sports such as paddleboarding and snorkeling.

Afternoon: Enjoy a delicious lunch at one of the beachfront restaurants or tavernas, savoring fresh seafood and traditional Greek dishes while taking in the mesmerizing sea views. Continue relaxing on the beach, soak up the sun, or embark on a leisurely walk along the coastline, exploring the nearby coves and fascinating rock formations.

Evening: As the day draws to a close, drive to the charming village of Pelekas, known for its breathtaking sunset vistas. Make your way to Kaiser's Throne, a viewpoint that offers panoramic views of the island and the shimmering sea. Witness the magical spectacle of the sunset as the sun dips below the horizon, painting the sky with vibrant hues. Afterward, enjoy a delightful dinner at a local taverna in Pelekas, such as Jimmy's Restaurant, and sample authentic Corfiot cuisine.

Day 3: Cultural and Historical Exploration

Morning: After breakfast, embark on a cultural journey to Achilleion Palace, a beautiful neoclassical palace built by Empress Elisabeth of Austria (Sisi). Explore the palace's opulent rooms, adorned with exquisite furnishings and artwork, and wander through the stunning gardens, featuring impressive statues and manicured landscapes. Learn about the history and significance of the palace through informative exhibits and guided tours.

Afternoon: Continue your cultural exploration with a visit to Mon Repos Estate, located near the Kanoni area. This former royal residence now serves as a museum and park, offering a glimpse into Corfu's rich history. Explore the neoclassical villa, which houses the Museum of Palaiopolis-Mon Repos, and delve into the island's archaeological heritage. Take a leisurely stroll through the estate's lush gardens, enjoying the serene atmosphere and the beauty of the surrounding nature.

Evening: Drive to the coastal village of Benitses and immerse yourself in its charming ambiance. Enjoy a delicious dinner at a seafood restaurant, such as Psaraki or Klimataria, savoring fresh catches of the day, including grilled fish, calamari, and seafood pasta.

Day 4: Adventure and Outdoor Activities

Morning: Start your day with an exhilarating horseback riding adventure in the scenic village of Avlaki. Visit Trailriders Corfu and embark on a guided horseback riding tour through olive groves, forests, and along the coastline, experiencing the beauty of Corfu's countryside and enjoying the tranquility of nature.

Afternoon: Head to Agni Bay, a tranquil and picturesque bay known for its crystal-clear waters and abundant marine life. Rent snorkeling equipment and explore the underwater world, encountering colorful fish, sea urchins, and starfish. For those seeking more adrenaline-pumping activities, engage in water sports such as paddleboarding, kayaking, and jet skiing.

Evening: Conclude your adventurous day with a delightful seafood dinner at one of the waterfront restaurants in Agni Bay, such as Toula's Seaside or Nikolas Taverna. Savor fresh seafood dishes while enjoying the serene views of the bay and the gentle lapping of the waves.

Day 5: Island Hopping and Boat Tour

Morning: Embark on a full-day boat tour to the nearby islands of Paxos and Antipaxos, discovering the hidden gems of the Ionian Sea. Depart from Corfu Town or the port of Gaios and sail across the turquoise waters, enjoying the refreshing sea breeze and stunning coastal scenery. Visit the Blue Caves of Paxos and marvel at the breathtaking rock formations and vibrant blue waters.

Afternoon: Arrive at Antipaxos and spend time on the island's pristine beaches, such as Voutoumi Beach and Vrika Beach. Swim in the crystal-clear waters, relax on the sandy shores, and soak up the idyllic surroundings. Enjoy a picnic lunch on the beach or dine at one of the local tavernas, savoring fresh seafood and local delicacies.

Evening: Return to Corfu in the late afternoon and head back to your accommodation to freshen up. Enjoy a leisurely dinner at a restaurant in Corfu Town, such as Avli or Salto Wine Bar and Bistro, savoring delicious Mediterranean cuisine and reflecting on your island-hopping adventure.

Day 6: Traditional Villages and Scenic Drives

Morning: After breakfast, embark on a scenic drive to the village of Paleokastritsa, renowned for its stunning beaches, crystal-clear waters, and the historic Monastery of Paleokastritsa. Visit the monastery, perched on a hill overlooking the bay, and explore its beautiful gardens, chapels, and museum. Spend some time on the beaches of Paleokastritsa, swimming, sunbathing, and snorkeling in the turquoise waters.

Afternoon: Continue your journey with a scenic drive to Angelokastro, a Byzantine castle located on a steep hilltop with panoramic views of the island. Explore the ancient ruins of the castle, imagining its historical significance, and take in the breathtaking vistas of the coastline and surrounding landscapes. Enjoy lunch at a local taverna in the nearby village of Lakones, savoring traditional Greek dishes and admiring the stunning views.

Evening: Head to the charming fishing village of Kassiopi and experience its laid-back ambiance and picturesque harbor. Enjoy a delicious dinner at a waterfront restaurant, such as Trilogia or Kima Taverna, savoring fresh seafood and Mediterranean cuisine while taking in the harbor views.

Day 7: Relaxation and Farewell

Morning: After breakfast, drive to the village of Sidari on the northern coast of Corfu, known for its unique rock formations and the famous Canal d'Amour. Visit the Canal d'Amour, a natural channel carved by the sea through sandstone cliffs, and swim in the clear waters, exploring the fascinating rock formations. Spend some time on Sidari Beach, relaxing on the golden sands and enjoying the vibrant atmosphere.

Afternoon: Return to Corfu Town and enjoy a leisurely lunch at a local restaurant, such as The Venetian Well or Pomo D'Oro. Spend the afternoon shopping for souvenirs and local products in the charming boutiques and markets of the Old Town. Visit specialty food stores to purchase items such as kumquat products, olive oil, honey, and traditional sweets, taking home a taste of Corfu.

Evening: Conclude your Corfu adventure with a farewell dinner at a fine dining restaurant in Corfu Town, such as Etrusco or The White House Restaurant. Reflect on your wonderful experiences on the island, savoring a delicious meal and cherishing the memories you've created.

Night: Depending on your flight schedule, transfer to Corfu International Airport for your departure. Bid farewell to Corfu, taking with you cherished memories of your unforgettable 7-day journey on this captivating island.

Budgeting for Your Trip

Flights to Corfu

Budget Airlines: €50–€150 for round-trip flights from major European cities.
Regular Airlines: €150–€300 depending on season and booking time.

Accommodation

Hostels/Budget Hotels: €20–€50 per night.
Mid-Range Hotels: €60–€120 per night.
Luxury Resorts/Villas: €150–€400 per night.

Transportation

Public Buses: €1.50–€3 per trip.
Car Rental: €30–€50 per day.
Scooter/ATV Rental: €15–€25 per day.
Taxis: €10–€30 depending on distance.

Food and Dining

Street Food: €3–€5 per meal.
Tavernas: €10–€20 per person.
Fine Dining: €30–€60 per person.

Activities and Sightseeing

Beaches: Free access; sunbed rentals €5–€10 per day.
Cultural Sites
Old Fortress: €6.
Achilleion Palace: €8.
Mon Repos Estate: €4.

Boat Tours: €20–€50 depending on duration.
Water Sports: €15–€50.

Sample 7-Day Budget

Budget Traveler (€50–€70/day)

Flights: €100
Accommodation: €25 x 7 nights = €175
Transportation: €30
Food: €15 x 7 days = €105
Activities: €40
Miscellaneous: €30
Total: €480–€520

Mid-Range Traveler (€100–€150/day)

Flights: €150
Accommodation: €90 x 7 nights = €630
Transportation: €70
Food: €30 x 7 days = €210
Activities: €70
Miscellaneous: €50
Total: €1,180–€1,330

Luxury Traveler (€200–€400/day)

Flights: €250
Accommodation: €250 x 7 nights = €1,750
Transportation: €150
Food: €60 x 7 days = €420
Activities: €150
Miscellaneous: €100
Total: €2,820–€3,270

Printed in Great Britain
by Amazon